Supplier Certification –
A Continuous
Improvement Strategy

SUPPLIER CERTIFICATION – A CONTINUOUS IMPROVEMENT STRATEGY

Richard A. Maass, John O. Brown, and
James L. Bossert

Customer-Supplier Technical Committee
American Society for Quality Control

Supplier Certification —
A Continuous Improvement Strategy

Richard A. Maass
John O. Brown
James L. Bossert

Library of Congress Cataloging-in-Publication Data

Bossert, James L.
    Supplier certification : a continuous improvement strategy / James L.
Bossert, John O. Brown, and Richard A. Maass.
      p. cm.
    Includes bibliographical references.
    ISBN 0-87389-083-3
    1. Quality control.   2. Industrial procurement.   I. Brown, John O.
II. Maass, Richard A.   III. Title.
TS156.B665   1989
658.5'62–dc20   89-18105
                                                  CIP

Copyright ©1990 by ASQC Quality Press

ISBN 0-87389-083-3

10 9 8 7 6 5 4 3 2 1

Acquisitions Editor: Jeanine L. Lau
Production Editor: Tammy Griffin
Cover design by Artistic License. Set in Zapf International by DanTon Typographers.
Printed and bound by BookCrafters.

Printed in the United States of America

Quality Press, American Society for Quality Control
310 West Wisconsin Avenue, Milwaukee, Wisconsin 53203

DEDICATED
TO
RICHARD A. "RICK" MAASS
(1930 – 1988)

For his years of faithful contributions to the Customer-Supplier Technical Committee, diligent pursuit of excellence in the customer-supplier relationship, and his vast literary contribution to the development and assimilation of this text, we dedicate this book to his memory.

Contents

Preface

Supplier certification is one of the more focused processes to hit the quality area in the past few years. This stems from the fact that most companies have traditionally focused improvement efforts on the internal functions of their operations. The growth of their products' value caused a series of questions to come up. These were along the lines of, "How do we get control over those suppliers who are killing us?" The revolution came when it was realized that inspection and more inspection was not the answer. Just as the plants' assurance systems internally changed to process controls and predictive actions, the way to work with suppliers had to change.

Supplier certification practices as described in this book have been repeatedly demonstrated to work and work well. Some of the contributors to the original discussions have cut inspection of purchased materials by 40% or more. One of the authors was involved in a plant startup where the redundant cost of receiving inspections was completely avoided by active work with suppliers.

The most successful applications are those where the entire supplier-customer relationship is undergoing change. It is in the partnerships where cost, quality, and delivery agreements are fostered that certification works best. The full partnership where each party is a stakeholder in each other's success is the aim. Supplier certification actions can be a launching pad to learning this environment.

Acknowledgments

As with all works, many people joined together to develop the ideas combined in this volume. Individual listing of such a collaborative effort is too long to print here, but there are key people we wish to recognize.

Arletta Maass has been first and foremost in our minds as we took her late husband's concepts and outlines to completion. Without her enthusiastic help in pulling together notes, contacts, and partially completed text sections, we could never have finished the work. Many thanks to her.

The original Customer-Supplier Technical Committee, who united to brainstorm the concepts and practices and made the presentations at the 1988 Annual Quality Congress, must be acknowledged as the real experts behind this effort. We have acted only as transcribers of their good works.

Several others who aided in the creation of this work include: Joe Grott, Mary Beth Wood, and Daryl Matthews, who helped with several reviews and offered many editorial suggestions. Also, Jerry Krahula's personal experience contributed greatly to Chapter 12, *Decertification and Recovery.* Additional thanks go to Jeanine Lau for her confidence and patience in working with us.

James L. Bossert
John O. Brown

Introduction

The most significant recent innovation in the customer-supplier interface is a program called *Certification of Suppliers*. A certified supplier is a source that, through previous experience and qualification, can provide material of such quality that it needs little, if any, receiving inspection or test before becoming approved stock or being released into the production process. The concept has rapidly spread through many industries and currently interests many ASQC members. However, like many new and different programs, supplier certification has developed with some confusion. This work follows the steps to implementation of certification — not through theory, but through a "nuts and bolts" approach.

Material herein represents the best thinking of the ASQC Customer-Supplier Technical Committee members, who deal daily with supplier certification. The ASQC Customer-Supplier Technical Committee was chartered 25 years ago to explore, debate, and publish issues and answers in the broad area of customer-supplier relationships.

Both customers and suppliers were represented in the group that contributed to this text's explanatory effort. While this work is not intended as a follow-up to *Procurement Quality Control* (4th edition, edited by Bossert)[1], it can be used as such. That text contains the basic steps necessary to set up a Supplier Program.

Following Chapter 1, which contains definitions, descriptions, and identification of sources with certification potential, the book progresses to the approved supplier stage — precertification — to define the necessary procedure to attain the certification threshold. Each succeeding chapter covers a significant phase of that process. Inclusion of case studies, "war stories," and checklists should contribute to the reader's understanding of the procedure. Benefits and the association of supplier certification with modern management forms conclude the effort.

The authors are confident that a study of these techniques will contribute to the success of a newly formed program or the improvement of an existing effort. Always remember that supplier certification was designed as a quality improvement program but will be a significant factor in your company's survival in the quality required by the future.

Lewis Carroll's *Through the Looking Glass* demonstrates what we may believe management wants when instructed to install a supplier certification program. Alice was told that she had to do it all, with each item being done first. We hope

Supplier Certification — A Continuous Improvement Strategy offers you more guidance than the White Rabbit gave Alice.

We all know we must start somewhere and not everywhere at once as Alice was advised. Getting started is the easy part. The major challenge comes with continuing on to maturity and attaining improvements from your poorer suppliers. That is when you will realize you truly have reached "Wonderland."

Reference

1. ASQC Customer-Supplier Technical Committee. *Procurement Quality Control,* 4th ed. James L. Bossert, editor. Milwaukee: ASQC Quality Press, 1988.

Introduction to Certification

Certification of suppliers is the answer to many customer-supplier problems. It may be the only answer to getting the supplier into a just-in-time (JIT) inventory system, where the supplier-furnished material is brought into the customer's facility just in time to go into the process or onto the assembly line. It also is attractive when considering the reduction of quality costs related to incoming inspection and test.

But, as someone once said, "There is no such thing as a free lunch." A program to truly select, elevate, and use certified suppliers is difficult, time-consuming, and expensive. Yes, the rewards at the end of the rainbow are comprehensive and long lasting, but do not think of supplier certification as a cheap fix; it is not.

Many individuals, particularly those in segments of manufacturing management other than quality, have failed to recognize the deep-seated implications of certification. There are so-called programs where suppliers have been selected simply on the basis of volume or cost. Those suppliers were called to a meeting, informed that they had been blessed with the title of "Certified," and then told not to make any more mistakes and that's it!

Those programs have little potential for success. When programs fail, the unenlightened people who formulated them discover they have simply transferred the problem from one pocket to another. Instead of an incoming lot failure costing one incoming inspector or laboratory technician's time and a flurry of paperwork to return the material, the company now faces the cost of 37 people sitting idle on a production line awaiting new material. The result is a ruptured distribution schedule. Obviously, that problem transferred from one pocket to the other has multiplied the dollars involved manyfold.

Now that we have explained what a certified supplier is not, let's define what a certified supplier is:

> *A certified supplier is one who, after extensive investigation, is found to supply material of such quality that it is not necessary to perform routine testing on each lot received.*

This is the definition formulated and adopted by PMA, the Pharmaceutical Manufacturers Association. We believe it fairly states the premise for all forms of industry, particularly those engaged in the manufacturing of a product. Just as other quality function techniques have been tailored, and in some cases improved, for application to service industries, it is logical that certification could be so used, although at the time of this writing little has been attempted in this field.

It should be understood that certification is not what has been traditionally called an *approved supplier* — which is the first stage for a new source. Certification implies a much higher quality level and experience. In some industries, particularly automotive, they even have a middle level called *preferred* or *target* suppliers. Those are approved sources who have performed well and should be given first chance at new contracts or special opportunities over approved sources, but they may or may not be certified. That is, their material may or may not go into stock without full inspection.

The members of the Customer-Supplier Technical Committee believe there are certain characteristics that prevail among suppliers who are successfully certified. The list sounds much like the hero companies Tom Peters cites in his book, *In Search of Excellence*.[1] Every supplier will have more or less of each desirable quality but will assuredly have most of these attributes.

The successful supplier will have a *new culture* management philosophy, and be aware of the future. He will be prepared to share his customer's goals, commitments, and even risks to promote a long-term relationship. The supplier we seek knows his own quality, is continuously looking for improvement, and is open to advice on how *zero defects* can be achieved. He can provide conforming product without excessive sorting or blending, even at the early stages of development, because his measurement system can define good, bad, and marginal.

Naturally, he ranks high on the customer's supplier rating system, usually at a 95% to 100% performance level. The supplier also has his own purchased material quality program, at least as close to complete as the customer's, to assure that he has the proper material or service base to start making product. He is capable of contributing technical expertise at the product design stage. Ordinarily, this supplier requires minimum attention from the customer and solves his own problems if possible, but when the need arises, he communicates skillfully and responds in a timely manner. He loves his product and he loves his people, and that means having good labor relations.

The supplier who should be considered for certification is also a good business associate. His product arrives in the correct time frame and in good physical condition. There are no extreme price fluctuations. After all, what is the use of expending effort to certify if the source is about to be eliminated because of late delivery or excessive profit-taking?

While this is difficult to quantify, perhaps above all, the supplier engenders a feeling of trust by the customer's purchasing group, by the design and operation engineers, and by the quality assurance function. He can truly be considered an extension of the customer's factory.

> *The supplier who should be considered for certification is also a good business associate.*

Based on these definitions and descriptions, a decision must be made whether the cultivation and elevation of these sources would be to the advantage of the customer company. Make sure the decision is made by all who will be affected. Once begun, the program must be carried out with no interruptions. There is no room for weak-hearted managers in this type of process. This obviously includes those at top operations management, who must fund the program, but also means commitment from purchasing, planning and scheduling, and various engineering functions, both design and development, production, and every part of the quality function. The last discipline, production, sounds like it might be assumed, but if the management of the prevention group and the management of the appraisal group have different ambitions and goals, the program could become chaotic. This, of course, results in a rise in the third point of the quality triangle, failure costs. Require a standing and resounding "Yes" from each group involved.

Discussion

One of the members of the Customer-Supplier Technical Committee related the following story to the authors when we were brainstorming about the contents of this book:

A boss two levels above him had attended many presentations about the new supplier certification program his company was quietly installing. All of the details of working in concert with suppliers to gain true capability by changing processes and some product specifications had been reviewed in great detail. Estimates of six months at a minimum to review supplier histories and where they were with respect to these new criteria were given before key suppliers were to be chosen for the new program. An additional six months for documenting the processes was given to the management teams at the kickoff meetings. Presentations had taken place during three consecutive weeks in September.

Approximately three weeks into the launch of the program during the reviews of supplier history, rejects, and line problems, an executive approached our associate and said that he wanted six suppliers certified in the next eight weeks. Our associate was taken by surprise because it was obvious that the executive had missed the point of the entire set of presentations. Our associate thought about the statement for a few minutes and had to reply the only way he could. He told him that the executive would have to talk to the parts involved as they were not cooperating with the program and that they did not get any better just because the program was started. He explained to the executive that the parts were the same as they were three weeks back — not to specification.

We believe that this one true story relates how critical it is that top management have a full understanding that a certification program is not going to improve the quality levels in the short run. It is a long, slow process. The start of a program is just that, a start, and that is all. It is not a panacea. Without measurement and known quality levels at the program's initiation, it will not by and of itself improve the acceptance levels.

Reference

1. Peters, Tom. *In Search of Excellence*. New York: Random House, 1979.

Supplier Approval, Measurement

In Chapter 1 we provided a detailed definition of a certified supplier. Now in Chapter 2 we are going to discuss the approval process required to become an *Approved Supplier* as a lead-in to certification. This chapter will also explain how the approval process is implemented for a new supplier and an existing supplier. To establish a firm foundation of the process, we will provide you with a few detailed definitions and a model of the process.

Approved Supplier: A supplier who has met minimum qualification criteria and has been approved to supply a required item. Customer inspection and testing would precede use.

Preferred Supplier: An approved supplier who is actively participating in the certification process. Typically his quality history is excellent. He may pull samples for customer testing and provide lot-specific certificates of analysis for the required item. The customer may be operating with reduced testing.

Certified Supplier: A supplier who, after extensive investigation, is found to supply material of such quality that it is not necessary to perform routine testing on each lot received.

Many purchasing departments have traditionally approved suppliers on price only. If we are to reach the ultimate partnership concept we propose here, this needs to be expanded a great deal. Full purchasing approval should now include the concepts of delivery, management linkage, and support for future projects or expansion. These suppliers would then become the core of the total supply base that the purchasing departments want to see business grow with and would want to do business with in five to ten years. The suppliers you wish to be in partnership with far into the future are considered preferred. This would give us three levels of suppliers when the supplier control system is fully implemented. *Approved* being those you can continue to purchase material from, *preferred* suppliers being those you want to do more business with, and *certified* being those who have met or exceeded all your quality program requirements. Figure 2.1 shows the breakdown into these three categories of one company's supply base of 600 suppliers. The numbers represent a program that is in its seventh year. The certification program can be considered mature when five to 20 suppliers per year become certified.

Understanding if your present suppliers are *approved* by all the appropriate functions involved depends mostly on your supplier performance measurement system. If you have been measuring performance based on the following criteria and have been making source selection/deselection based on this type of measurement, then there is a high probability that you already have approved suppliers. If not, a supplier performance measurement system should be developed that will allow you to start making decisions based on hard data. As you set up or use the system to make choices on which suppliers are *approved*, you can generate a supplier list which the purchasing function will use to guide business decisions.

The key criteria in rating a supplier's performance described here are the results of working with suppliers ranging from the largest corporation to the small shop down the street. These criteria were developed to provide for not only a means for the purchasing company to measure its suppliers but also so the departments within that company have a means of communication.

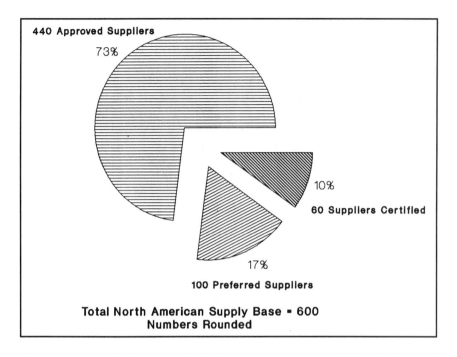

440 Approved Suppliers
73%

10%
60 Suppliers Certified

17%
100 Preferred Suppliers

Total North American Supply Base = 600
Numbers Rounded

Figure 2.1   Supply base analysis for one company with breakdown of approved, preferred, and certified suppliers.

Five criteria are widely agreed on:

1. **Quality**

   This involves levels of conformance to a standard. What is the standard and how do you measure a supplier's level of conformance? The important fact is that you measure your suppliers consistently and report regularly in a data-based manner. The measure must be against a known standard of performance that is agreed to by all users or consumers of the product delivered.

2. **Delivery**

   Measures of on-time delivery are becoming imperative as change comes to various industries. *Just-in-time* deliveries and *ship-to-use* programs will only work if suppliers are measured on their performance to the set objectives. To properly balance this measure, lead times and consistent order quantities need to be reinforced internally. If the internal disciplines are in place a "measure of delivery" capability will be developed already, but the data may not be generated or used.

3. **Technical Support**

Technical support is not a criterion that is easily defined. It is heavily dependent on industry product and process. We usually include here the engineering talent and how it is used by the supplier. Does the supplier's engineering group or its equivalent become involved during the bid phase or later? Does the supplier's engineering group suggest improvements in the product or process? Are the engineers present and providing input at all phases of the relationship? What is important is not whether the measure is objective or subjective but rather that it is made. The technical support provided must be measured; without measurement there is no base for evaluating the future program potential of a supplier.

4. **Management Attitude**

How to measure the attitude of a supplier's management is a stumbling block for most of us in business today. Suggestions that are helpful here are in the areas of responsiveness, interest demonstrated in your end product and its consumers, ongoing communications, and demonstration of a partnership relationship. Experience shows that the closer to a partnership you are with a supplier, the higher you will rate a supplier in this area. This is closest to an overall composite of all our interactions with suppliers. Measuring management attitude is the hardest, but it is the most critical of all. Without this measure you can have product delivered on time, on cost to the specification, but have your supply cut off tomorrow with no previous notification.

5. **Cost**

Many companies still look at cost as only purchased cost. The true cost of a purchased commodity needs to include the extraordinary cost of handling, service, inspection, and lost production time because of rejects. Ideally, if there were none of the extraordinary costs invoked, the supplier would be truly the low cost supplier. If you set up a system to measure true cost, then your purchasing department becomes your ally in measuring because you are in effect measuring its ongoing performance as well.

To summarize, if you measure suppliers against quality, technical support, management attitude, delivery, and cost, you will have a more than fair judge of performance from which you can launch improvement processes, which could lead to a preferred supplier. Companies that exhibit characteristics that measure well against this type of broad-based system will be those that are to become your certified suppliers without a doubt. They demonstrate the application of the characteristics that Tom Peters[1] held forth in his hero companies, and will be the willing partners in a quality certification process.

Up to now, we have assumed that your supply base is well-established and what was needed was a measurement system to discover which suppliers were those you wanted to do more business with in the future. You are still faced with the problem of adding a supplier to that group, or new supplier approvals. There are a few basic steps that need to be taken to get a new supplier on-line. Previously, they were usually performed within companies in isolation by the separate functions of purchasing and engineering. To support a partnership relationship this needs to change. Many companies have gone to doing new supplier approvals by a team made up of at least purchasing, engineering, and quality. The steps to new supplier approval can be as follows:

1. A joint review of a quote proposal is made by the team to assure that the new suppliers who are to quote have a complete package of specifications and requirements on which to base their quote.

2. All quotes that come back to your company are reviewed by purchasing for exceptions to the requirements. If there are exceptions or alternates offered to the specification package, a team review is required to establish if the quote is valid. If it is, then a site visit is warranted.

3. The team performs a quality systems survey of the proposed new supplier. This assesses whether the supplier has a basic overall quality program that could control the manufacturing of the product quoted on.

4. An order for engineering samples would then be made to the supplier. These samples would be fully tested and measured by both the quality functions and the engineering functions based on the specifications given to the supplier. In some industries this is called an initial sample run, preproduction, or prototype run. The important point is that the samples are fully documented and a technical report on the results of inspections and tests by all involved parties is generated.

5. The supplier should provide, with the samples, an estimate of his capability in an agreed on statistical summary.

6. Assuming steps 1 to 5 have given acceptable results, the supplier should now be released to manufacture product that matches or exceeds the results of the samples. This release would be given by the team that did the survey, the inspections, and the engineering tests. Only then could the supplier be added to an approved supplier list for additional business.

Without a measurement system to determine where your current suppliers are performance-wise, or a system for adding new suppliers to the approved supplier list, it is not possible to launch a supplier certification program. The building blocks for certification are in the knowledge and understanding of where the supplier's performance is and how that performance was measured.

In support of step 3 there is a worldwide movement of supplier systems approval by third party audits. In many countries there are either government or trade associations that are approving or performing registration of companies' quality systems to various standards. The basis of this system is usually an audit against an international or national standard such as the ISO 9000[2] or ANSI/ASQC Q90 series standards.[3] In some newly industrialized countries and socialist countries the standards are issued by the government. In the United Kingdom, for example, the British Standards Institute is performing audits against the requirements of BS5750[4] (their version of the ISO 9000 series). They then provide lists of the companies that have met the requirements to those who ask.

This type of system will be extended to most industrialized countries. The acceptance of centralized audits by potential customers is, as of this writing, mixed. In some industries the acceptance of this type of audit to a published standard will far exceed the needs for a basic quality system. In others it will not meet the basic needs and will need to be at least supplemented with an on-site audit against the higher level requirements needed. Over time there will be a reduction in redundant audits for the same basic systems. By taking advantage of agency audits for the initial quality systems qualification, you can spend more time on the task of understanding the specific product control system you will be developing to work toward certification of your suppliers.

. . . unless you spend the time and effort to establish where your supply base is in relation to your current needs, it becomes difficult to start a supplier certification program.

In conclusion, unless you spend the time and effort to establish where your supply base is in relation to your current needs, it becomes difficult to start a supplier certification program. We recommend spending the time to research this area as the findings will usually surprise you. You will find that quite a few of your suppliers are already in the preferred classification. It is with those suppliers you should start a certification process, because you will get early successes and the best return on the time invested. You can then move on to working with those suppliers who need the most improvement, because management will be realizing the benefits that will come with expanding the program.

References

1. Peters, Tom. *In Search of Excellence.* New York: Random House, 1979.

2. ISO 9000-9004 1987 Series. *Quality Management and Quality Assurance Standards.* ISO/TC 176, 1987.

3. ANSI/ASQC Q90-1987 Series. *Quality Management and Quality Assurance Standards.* Milwaukee: American Society for Quality Control, 1987.

4. BS5750. *Quality Systems.* London: British Standards Institute, 1986.

General Certification Criteria

I
t is easy to make the decision to have a certification of suppliers program. It becomes a little harder to obtain management commitment and especially commitment of resources for such a program. But the hardest thing of all is to decide on the criteria for a certified supplier. There are usually as many opinions as there are people, plus two. After much debate and narrowing down, we have chosen eight specific criteria. The eighth topic, process control, is treated in two separate chapters (Chapters 4 and 5); one for the bulk process industry and one for the piece-part group. The general criteria include the following:

1. *Having virtually no product-related lot rejections for a significant time period, usually a calendar year or in some cases two years.* Some prefer to state the criteria in volume, i.e., no rejects in 20 consecutive lots, or 10 samplings of skip-lot inspection. Others use a fraction defective goal, i.e., less than 0.5% defective on all dimensions or attributes. All aim at the same thing — a benchmark of superior performance.

   No matter how you view it, the proof is in the product, so the supplier's track record must be considered. A good quality system produces consistently good lots. When a rejection or nonconformance occurs, it must be analyzed as to its severity, the corrective action taken, and the risk of repetition. An isolated incident, in which good corrective action has been implemented, and which probably will never happen again, must be viewed with less importance than the repetitive problem that creeps in every third lot or so. Decide on a risk assessment of the problem product's potential for creating an on-line process delay or field complaint due to poor quality. Perhaps the customer program administration still might be willing to certify the source if there is less than 1% chance of another incident, or if the fix only costs 12 cents.

   Don't get "bogged down" by the problem of making an exact risk assessment. Most of the time plain and available good judgment will dictate 99%, 90%, 75%, 50%, or 10% chance of a problem. If two people can argue whether the risk is 93.5% or 94%, you had better rethink the problem anyway.

2. *Having no nonproduct-related rejections for a stated period of time, usually six months.* Why should we separate product-related rejections, such as assay, dimensions, or color, from nonproduct-related rejections, such as the marking on the container, the timeliness of the analysis document, and others? After all, both kinds of requirements are part of the specification. The answer is, simply because they each require a different type of corrective action.

   If the assay of a process industry product fails, usually long and hard investigations are conducted, and one might well want to wait a full year or for many lots to be sure the composition problem is cured. A mismarked container usually requires the retraining of the person who makes the stencil. It would be unproductive to hold back an otherwise qualified supplier from certification until December for something he positively corrected last January. Again, a risk assessment is made relating to the danger of a repeat problem.

3. *Having no production-related negative incidents for a stated period of time, usually six months.* Incoming inspection and test determine conformance to specifications, but we all know the specification cannot define everything, or the document would be the size of a big city telephone book. Often, down in the factory, the production and quality control functions can form a different opinion of a supplier, based on the ease with which the supplier's product can be inserted into the process or the assembly.

Any problems, even unknowingly created by the supplier, should be resolved or seriously considered when making a certification judgment. Generally, the record of these incidents should be in the supplier file in the form of a memo, but it is often necessary at the time of certification consideration to poll the production people to check their memory banks.

One of the types of problems that may be revealed by this investigation is the *warehouse error*. Perhaps 100 containers of material are received. Incoming inspection takes its random sample and finds the product acceptable. But at the bottom of one pallet lies a single box that may or may not be correctly marked, which contains the wrong piece part! It was carelessly loaded on the pallet at the supplier's warehouse from the wrong stack.

Another problem, often associated with bulk material, involves aging. Just-in-time deliveries may not be part of the picture when minimum order quantity is a six-month supply. Certainly, it passed laboratory tests when it arrived, but now — six months later — the chemical is in the form of "rocks" and is difficult to dissolve. This phenomenon may be the result of poor packaging, adverse storage conditions, or even the way the material was shipped. Discuss the product with production, because they may have the only knowledge of a problem that should be corrected before certification.

While the production view may be the most pertinent, many precertification checklists also include a discussion with engineering and purchasing. If, for example, the potential certification source has proved they cannot support new design technology and therefore will receive no new contracts, or the source has the customer on allocation already and eventually must be replaced to assure adequate supply, the significant effort necessary for certification might be wasted.

4. *Having successfully passed a recent on-site quality system evaluation.* Generally, the on-site evaluation is a criterion for simple supplier approval, let alone certification. Perhaps some of your more prominent suppliers qualified under the *grandfather clause*, because they were good suppliers for ten years before the start of evaluations. Maybe you have not had a person in the supplier's facility since the last time he expanded, seven years ago. Companies do change. As a result of new technology, production methods are altered, but did the control of quality keep up with the increased productivity? If their methods haven't changed, perhaps your requirements have. Even if you haven't had a rejection lately, certification may be the appropriate time to thoroughly examine the supplier's quality system again, if only to reassure yourself that it is still working well.

Generally, recent means less than one year. These criteria require some planning early in the year. When planning the trip schedule, take into consideration who might be eligible for certification later in the period. It is frustrating to have a supplier ready to change status, but because of poor planning you cannot find the time, the funds, or a reason to travel to Idaho in late November.

5. *Having a totally agreed on specification.* An agreement on the specification is necessary at any level of quality required. However, when considering certification of a supplier, it is necessary to review the document again. Search out any possibly ambiguous phrases like *characteristic odor,* or *clear of contamination,* or *free of flash,* and make sure an agreement has been reached. Even better, mutually change the specification so it is understandable. Check for any notations as to standards so that the latest issue is stated. Finally, make sure every print called out in the body of the specification is current.

Now is the time to address the subject of manufacturability. One of the most effective ways to avoid defects is to make the piece part easier to produce within tolerance. Often a slightly marginal condition, which will produce good parts 98% of the time, can be made a sure thing by adjustment of the basic parameters.

6. *Having a fully documented process and quality system.* At the quality levels appropriate for certification, all changes, especially small ones, must be controlled. The only way to accomplish this is to have an accurate picture of where you are and where you are going process-wise. That, of course, requires extensive documentation. Part of that system description must include a program to ensure continuous improvement and/or a program to maintain the process in its present highly satisfactory form. Many customers believe certification is not an end in itself; it is a stepping off place to greater achievement. One important part of any quality improvement system should be cost control. If the quality is achieved, but at excessive cost, the supplier can still lose business and go bankrupt.

7. *Having the ability to furnish timely copies of certificates of analysis, inspection data, and test results.* Remember, under some regulatory schemes, you cannot skip completing the standard tests unless you have the supplier's documentation in your hand! After the rigorous demands of the other criteria stated, this one sounds easy — but it is not.

Actually to arrange for the data to be available at the customer's plant when the product is ready for test seems to be almost impossible for some supplier companies. The mail hardly seems to be the answer, as the letter comes five days after the truck has arrived. If the certification is sent with the regular shipment papers, somehow it ends up with the bill of lading and eventually it is found a month later in accounts payable.

New methods are becoming available, like telefax, electronic mail, and direct computer hookups. Some customers have gone so far as to provide and link up with the process control systems that will generate the required inspection, analysis, or test data. This allows the use of a shared data base of information.

Many customers with extensive experience in the certification arena do not require that dimensional data, for example, be sent with every piece part lot. They do, however, demand that it be available for perusal by the customer at any time. Those customers feel that since they have placed so much trust in the certified supplier already, it would be redundant to insist on a huge stack of papers to be reproduced each time material is sent.

A possible compromise used by some companies is that data accompany the first few lots for review. Later the supplier is told to keep them in the file. Then, as part of the preparation for a periodic audit, a quantity of parts from the most recent arrival is measured. While on site, the numbers are compared. Any significant difference, whether average or distribution, requires immediate corrective action. It could result in decertification for a while until the mystery is resolved. The point is, do not assume that the transfer of data is easy. It must be planned and tried before stating the supplier meets these criteria.

8. *A process that is stable and demonstrated as being in control.* Once the supplier's process has been demonstrated to be under control and process capability studies have shown its ability to consistently produce acceptable quality product, there may need to be a period of time for verification testing by both the customer and supplier. The extent of the time needs to be determined on a case by case basis. These criteria are so important that we will devote the next two chapters to its evaluation — first for bulk materials, then for piece parts.

It is important to understand that the criteria for certification must include an appraisal of the process or processes that produce the material — be it a bulk chemical or a piece part. Many certification schemes are built only on performance, the so-called track record. But what if the supplier has been sorting the product — culling out 25% defectives all through the performance evaluation period? Would you certify this supplier knowing that almost inevitably the *suffer and sort* will be neglected or poorly done, and you will be stuck with a poor lot? Would you elevate this supplier above others when you know intuitively that somehow you are paying for those 25% culls, even though it does not show up as a quality cost? The answer to the last two questions should be a resounding *No!*

In the same vein, there may be a process that is so unstable that the center of the distribution keeps bouncing around — sometimes high, sometimes low, occasionally in the middle. This is often a symptom of poor process setup. So far the bounces have stayed between the specification limits, but if you certify that supplier, just as surely as Murphy's law, the next bounce will be over the wall.

It is important that the supplier have a good track record. As a matter of fact, it is essential! However, to be sure of the credibility of that performance, evaluate the process that produces it.

These are the general criteria. Are they difficult? Yes, but attainable. And that is the way it should be for certification.

Another criterion often added to these quality-oriented issues, is delivery performance. When supplier certification is part of an overall JIT effort, planning and scheduling, purchasing, and the quality function can create a program that examines the supplier's ability to be on time. This is a legitimate relationship as one of the anticipated results of the certification effort is an uninterrupted flow of acceptable shipments.

. . .quality should never want to push delivery so hard that the supplier gets the impression you want him to ship regardless of quality.

Usually this criterion is judged from a program similar to supplier rating. The shipment is considered approved if it arrives within, for example, five days before and two days after the established date. Perhaps it is not rejected (returned to supplier) if outside these limits, but is considered a defective as far as delivery is concerned. A performance index of 98% might be required before certification is granted. Of course, in an ultimate JIT program, the span might be within two hours and 15 minutes before and six minutes after (and snowstorms are not included in the equation). Many of these schemes are much more complex than this example, and require extensive negotiation within the customer company, using techniques beyond the scope of this book.

The quality function must be careful regarding its participation in this program. If the late shipment was the result of poor scheduling in the supplier's plant or careless use of transportation, quality would be well-advised to remove themselves from the discussion and let those experts on both sides solve the problem. If for no other reason than that quality should never want to push delivery so hard that the supplier gets the impression you want him to ship regardless of quality. On the other hand, if the source could not make the date because of internal quality failures, customer quality must immediately join in and help.

4

Bulk Process Industries

Certification of a bulk material supplier presents some unique problems. Generally speaking, this material is produced in large batches, which at some point could be mixed or blended into an even larger homogeneous mass. Therefore, there is usually only one test result per lot per characteristic. While it is true that multiple tests should be made initially to prove lot homogeneity or uniformity, once the shipments have begun, only one result per test per lot is normal.

It follows then, that a supplier could be a major factor in a customer's material program having submitted only three, four, five, or six large lots per year. Now where does this leave the customer quality control man? All the advanced statistical process control (SPC) technology is usually based on analysis of large quantities of data as related to average, or some form of central tendency, and the shape and size of the distribution. We all are aware of the confidence we can place in the parameters of a distribution calculated from three or six data points. Depending on the way the dot-points lay, sometimes it is little confidence and other times it is none!

One successful approach to certification for bulk material is to concentrate on the compatibility of the supplier's test results and the customer's test results. The first step still would be to compare both supplier and customer's results against the specifications and tolerances. If both results, little as they are, show that the supplier seems to be able to easily meet the requirements, take some small comfort from that. Then attack the second issue. If the customer stops testing the product, can he believe the supplier's test results?

Take as many incoming lots as you have history, and for each test parameter, list the supplier's result, as taken from the submitted *Certificate of Analysis*, and the customer laboratory result for that same submitted lot. By the way, this implies that the customer has good paperwork discipline and can match certification to internal laboratory result.

Compare the listing of both results using a paired *t* test. At least five and usually ten pairs are necessary, but the more pairs the better the conclusion. The paired *t* test, which concentrates on the means of the test results, will indicate whether the two sets of data came from the same population. If so, it can be inferred that the results correlate, and that the customer can believe the supplier's results as he would believe his own. If not, it implies he must continue testing before acceptance to justify putting the product into his process.

It might also be appropriate to compare the two distributions, small as they are, for sameness of shape and size. Because we have so few samples, normality is difficult to prove, so one of the many nonparametric statistics such as Wilcoxen's Rank Test seems to be most successful.

When the results do not agree, there are several possible explanations. The first and most common is a simple bias between laboratories. If both sets of data seem to be normally gathered around an average — but the two averages are, say, three percentage points apart — the statistical test will show no agreement. A mutual discussion of test methods is in order here, and that may clear up the bias. Should the bias remain, but can be explained, and it can be proved that it will always be say, three percentage points apart, and both points are well away from the tolerance limit, perhaps certification can still be established, although close monitoring is necessary.

The second reason for lack of correlation could be a change in the product between final supplier packoff and customer incoming inspection. A typical example of this might be the moisture content or loss on drying test. Then a discussion of the material package integrity is appropriate. Maybe a better gasket on the drum lid could eliminate the difference between results.

The third reason is the most difficult. If the bias is because both sets of data have no pattern, both are essentially scatter diagrams. The assignable cause may be lack of homogeneity, and that should be investigated and corrective action taken, whether certification is achieved or not. Don't be comforted by the fact that recent results have all been within specification. An unstable process could explode in any direction — and before you know it.

But if the pairs correlate, you have a "win" situation. Depending on the regulatory atmosphere of your industry, you can discontinue most tests that you have correlated. A word of warning: Usually it is best to have at least one identification test remain, to protect against the shipping clerk error of sending the wrong product altogether. And, of course, check for shipping damage.

Some of the tests for normality and control suggested in the next chapter may be adapted to the bulk materials industry. If the lot or batch sizes are small enough and run frequently, the systems for piece part SPC will work for gathering the data needed to reach certification.

Depending on the criticality of the material, an audit schedule should be set up. Perhaps twice a year a sample will be taken from the incoming lot and submitted to the laboratory just like before certification. Maybe a sliding schedule would be appropriate three times the first year, twice the second year, and once a year thereafter. However, there is one important difference. A sample is taken, but the material goes into approved stock immediately, often before test results are known. If your certification is tied to a JIT program, you cannot interrupt the predetermined product flow for random audits.

> *An unstable process could explode in any direction — and before you know it.*

To monitor the continued correlation, continue to use the same statistical test. Add each subsequent audit result to the previous data assay, and perform the test again. A five-pair test becomes a six-pair, and the next audit becomes a seven-pair, etc.

A word of warning here. The supplier must be impressed with the caveat that he cannot change the process without notifying his customer! Even if the change is a significant improvement and certainly should be implemented, the difference might show up on the statistical analysis and cause the customer to think there is an out-of-control condition. A few of the larger companies making stock products may resist this rule. They might believe that it is their product and they will do what they want with it. If they do not have consideration for their customer's needs, perhaps they should not be certified and would thereby not gain the competitive advantage that goes along with certification.

Again, it must be emphasized that everyone would be happier if we had much more data to establish the relationship between customer and supplier. When that is not possible, such as when dealing with bulk materials, don't give up — there are ways to certify those suppliers.

Piece Part Industries

Besides the general criteria stated in Chapter 3, the certification requirement for piece part or assembly suppliers is a demonstration of SPC. Actually, it really is attainment of the quality levels necessary to compete in the future, but usually those levels can be obtained only by strict application of SPC. The product of a certified piece part or assembly supplier will be subjected to little or no incoming inspection and test before being put into approved stock. Therefore, it is imperative that the process that produces the piece part be virtually incapable of making a defective.

Statistical process control has recently become the big "buzz word" in American industry. It simply means the elimination or reduction of variation until a stable, predictable process is achieved that is compatible with the requirements or tolerances needed. The customer and the supplier must study key dimensions of selected components, making improvements as they interact, until they have a process and product that is so tightly controlled that the probability of a rejected lot is simply improbable!

Defects per Million

Before starting to examine the process, we should change our thinking from acceptable quality levels (AQL) to defects per million (DPM). Acceptable quality levels in the usual scale of 1%, 2%, and 4% must be changed to allowances of 100, 500, and maybe 2,500 DPM units produced. The change to DPM units tends to shake people away from the old AQL mentality.

The relationship between the DPM rates and a process capability index (PCI) is shown in Figure 5.1. Many industries thinking in terms of SPC have already made the move to thinking in relation to Cpk, with goals of 1.0, 1.33, or 2.0 for their suppliers. The shift in thinking to DPM is rather a shift in expression, not a quantum leap in capability required to meet the stated targets. This shift in thinking assumes a stable process, already in control. The relationship we are talking about is shown in Table 5.1

The AQL mentality indicated that there was some level of nonconformance which was acceptable to the customer. The classic definition of AQL was that point where it was less costly for the customer to sort out the defectives or repair the assemblies than it was for the supplier to (usually by sorting) assure against them being shipped. This philosophy stemmed from sampling technology. As the AQL approached zero, sampling tables would approach infinity or the sample size equals the lot size — the old 100% theory, which was never 100% effective anyway.

But the real breakthroughs came when they moved from incoming inspection to supplier certification as the control plans

There have been as many modifications to the AQL sampling systems as engineers doing the work. One of the concepts that began to approach the DPM thought process was the use of a C=0 number for the acceptance number. By not knowingly accepting any defectives these companies had started the application of the concepts of DPM. Several companies started using C=0 plans in the 1960s with much success. But the real breakthroughs came when they moved from incoming inspection to supplier certification as the control plans. We recognize the need for steps in the progression from incoming controls to certification, and offer a means to move receiving inspection to this basis as one step.

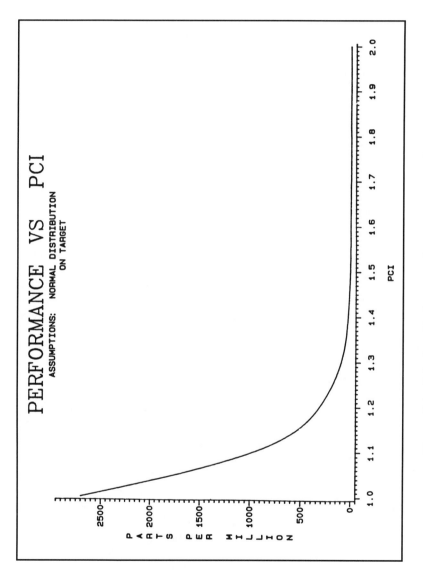

Figure 5.1   Relationship between the DPM rates and PCI.

Cpk/PCI	DPM	% DEFECTIVE
0.33	317,310	31.7
0.50	133,614	13.3
0.66	45,500	4.5
0.83	12,419	1.2
1.00	2,700	0.27
1.17	465	0.046
1.33	64	0.06
1.50	6.8	0.0007
1.66	0.6	0.00006
2.00	0.0018	0.00000018

*Note: There was some rounding done in these calculations to come closer to commonly used targets of Cpk and DPM.

Table 5.1   Comparative values of Cpk/PCI — DPM — % defective.

In a sample plan by Cross,[1] effectivity shows a good basic sample plan based on C=0 at different DPM targets (Table 5.2).

Actually, most AQLs were not set by an understanding of what the customer's process could cull out with little economic loss. The final figure was a negotiated settlement — often following a bitter fight — a compromise between the customer's desire for no defects and the supplier's *best guess* generated from his history, so-called industry standards, and loaded with an added *comfort factor.* In other words, neither side understood nor took the trouble to really figure out what the answer should be.

> *In the world of SPC and DPM units, the only acceptable target is no defects at all.*

In the world of SPC and DPM units, the only acceptable target is no defects at all. However, we as customers must be pragmatic practitioners! We know that by the laws of probability which govern the analysis of distributions, nothing is impossible, even if that probability is stated with a decimal point and 26 zeros. So bring the statistics out of the "closet," admit the possibility of an out of tolerance part, but put in the effort to reduce that "number" to such a low level that it has little or no impact on the quality output.

Are these minuscule levels really necessary? Only if your company wishes to compete and survive against aware entities who don't waste their profits on scrap, field failures, and warranty costs. These are the quality levels needed in the future, and it is the certified supplier who can furnish these levels.

LOT SIZE	500 ppm			250 ppm			100 ppm			50 ppm		
	n	c	pt%*	n	c	pt%	n	c	pt%	n	c	pt%
1-200	All	0	—	All	0	—	All	0	—	All	0	—
201-300	213	0	1.08	249	0	.92	277	0	.83	288	0	.80
301-400	259	0	.89	315	0	.73	361	0	.64	379	0	.61
401-500	298	0	.77	373	0	.62	440	0	.52	468	0	.49
501-600	330	0	.70	426	0	.54	516	0	.45	555	0	.41
601-800	383	0	.60	518	0	.44	657	0	.35	722	0	.32
801-1000	424	0	.54	595	0	.39	787	0	.29	880	0	.26
1001-2000	538	0	.43	848	0	.27	1295	0	.18	1572	0	.15
2001-3000	591	0	.39	987	0	.23	1652	0	.14	2131	0	.108
3001-4000	622	0	.37	1076	0	.21	1916	0	.12	2591	0	.089
4001-5000	641	0	.36	1137	0	.20	2120	0	.108	2977	0	.077
5001-7000	666	0	.35	1216	0	.19	2412	0	.095	3587	0	.064
7001-10,000	685	0	.34	1283	0	.18	2690	0	.086	4239	0	.054
10,001-20,000	710	0	.32	1371	0	.17	3107	0	.074	5379	0	.043
20,001-50,000	725	0	.32	1430	0	.16	3426	0	.067	6414	0	.036
50,001-100,000	730	0	.32	1450	0	.16	3548	0	.065	6854	0	.034

*pt% = Lot Tolerance Percent Defective (LTPD)

Table 5.2 Parts per million AQL sampling plans for 500, 250, 100, and 50 ppm (Cross¹).

Studies of processes at this level should start at the beginning. To accomplish this, we must move the quality decision back. Experience has shown that it is usually fruitless to only attack the final process that produces the piece part. More often than not, most of the trouble is already built in. To get to DPM, you must start your SPC program at the design board, die, mold, or machine tool! The operator is a variable that must be included in the studies, and therefore must be included at the start of the program.

Statistical Process Control

The part design should take into consideration all the knowledge accumulated when making similar components. Guard against a design that requires plus or minus one thousandths to function, when the best your supplier has ever previously attained was plus or minus five (or in SPC language, a process capability of ten thousandths). With the help of the supplier, make the configuration as easy to produce as possible. This is called manufacturability. At the conceptual stage, significant changes can be made by adjusting the thinking of the creator. Don't wait until later, when the tolerance may be frozen by interaction with mating parts.

This means taking the initial data in a representative manner from a single run, single machine, single operator mode, usually at the *prove out* stage. This approach is significantly different from many SPC programs. They start at the final product stage, using data obtained from an $\bar{X}$ *and* R chart over a fairly long period, to obtain the data to examine the process. We must respectfully disagree with that technique, for as Neiswanger[2] strongly stated as early as 1951, "When time is a factor, data ceases to be homogeneous. . .data affected by time is not suited to frequency-distribution analysis." This author, who never has received much recognition in the quality assurance field because he wrote mainly about marketing statistics, certainly understood the use of timely data.

The first thing to be studied is process capability. When the brand new mold is given a trial, determine from the measurements how wide the distribution of values will be for any particular dimension. Therein lies the biggest difference from our present technology. Today we deal principally with the average — not the distribution. The average result, of course, is important, but only as it relates to the width of the distribution and the tolerance band or spread. From the trial run, find the process capability and express it in an important nomenclature called *capability ratio*. The simple formula is six times the standard deviation, divided by the total tolerance spread. The relationship between process width and tolerance spread is now established.

It is important to test the distribution for normality — that is, the shape of the curve. We are looking for symmetry, not too flat, not too peaked. Chi-square, skew, and kurtosis are the usual statistical tests. The reason we need this assurance of shape is because we know a lot about curves that pass the test for normality. How much area or percentage of the normal curve lies between certain widths is well-known, and stated in exact numbers in tables. However, if the curve turns out to be slightly less than normal, don't panic! There are also many ways to deal with nonparametric distributions. As long as it is stable and can be depended on to reproduce its shape, it can be controlled.

If it is totally abnormal — literally a scatter diagram — now panic! Actually, what a scatter diagram usually means is the process is changing within itself, and is not yet ready to be studied. Try to remove any changing conditions, and run another test. It probably has settled down to a readable pattern. If not, you must try again! Studying a process before it gels is like trying to read a telephone book before the names have been alphabetized. Another possibility for the scatter is a lack of test precision. Chapter 6 addresses the importance of precision, accuracy, and gathering of data.

Next we study the average — the arithmetic center of the process. Often the two companion pieces — median and mode — are also determined, but mostly to examine the shape of the distribution. We must relate the average to the design center. Please notice the words *design center*, the midpoint between the tolerance limits. Many design engineers will create a tolerance something like "plus two thousandths, minus ten thousandths" in an effort to show there is more danger in being too big than too small. When doing an SPC study, however, and dealing with normal curves, the midpoint is far more important to us.

The relationship of the average and the design center is expressed as the *location ratio*, calculated by dividing the difference between the two by one half of the tolerance spread. In some processes, it is thought that the nominal is not significant and therefore is not specified. In this situation, only the upper and lower tolerance are considered important. In SPC technology, nevertheless, a midpoint must be calculated if only to determine the relationship of the average to the edge.

Even more popular is the use of the technique which results in Cpk indices. The Cpk number combines both location and spread factors and helps make the same decision of fitness for use. The number most often set as the target is a process that can show a Cpk of 1.33. In some situations, related to a critical variable — one that if it fails could be injurious to life — customers demand a Cpk of 2.0 or better. This Cpk is certainly an acceptable statistical technique if both customer and supplier agree that it will be their statement of process control.

. . . it is important that these design and process engineers and their managers understand the concept if you expect them to help you. . .

The previously explained two-ratio system (capability ratio and location ratio), however, has been found to be easier to teach than Cpk to those who are not quality engineers. And it is important that these design and process engineers and their managers understand the concept if you expect them to help you with the corrective action necessary to bring the process under an SPC regime. Another somewhat less popular technique is to make the decision of acceptability on the basis of Z scores. The Z score is simply half the tolerance spread divided by the calculated standard deviation of the process. At least 3.0 and more, usually 4.0, are acceptable results. This system, however, seems to be weak in that it often does not appreciate the impact of the relationship of the nominal and average.

It is not necessary to show process capability on each and every tooling dimension. Facets to be examined must be those essential to the function of the part and those affecting the handling or assembly of the part. The selection of dimensions to be studied should be a mutual decision made by the customer and supplier — the one who knows how it is made and the one who knows how it is used. This may call for a characteristic criticality classification system to be used on more complex products.

If the supplier furnishes many parts of similar configuration, it may not be necessary to study each unit during the initial phases of the program. Select *worst cases* and nominals for the first study. Perhaps the biggest, the smallest, and two in the middle. Certainly, however, include those that have a history of dimensional problems. Eventually, all piece parts from the supplier will have to be studied, usually before supplier certification status is granted. However, start your analysis with an important few. It is our experience that a thorough review of some well-illuminated problems and solutions associated with these few pieces studied then can be applied to the many remaining, even before analysis is performed.

Before the program starts, select your SPC targets. Remember, this is a long-term program. You may not be able to go right to the ultimate target that you desire — 150 DPM units. Maybe you will start with a target of 650 DPM units for this year, and work your way down as the need for greater quality becomes evident. About one fourth to one third of the present AQL might be an appropriate first-time target. This is, after all, an initial study of a *frozen* process. The extra room will allow for later, hopefully slight, inprocess variations introduced by time, wear, machine changes, etc. Select your initial SPC targets on the basis of criticality, or cost of failure. While we all hope to have every part to the 150 DPM level in the future, maybe we can live with 2,500 DPM on a simple corrugated box for a while, as we concentrate our resources on parts where the cost of failure is thousands of dollars. The situation of having a critical part at a level of 5,000 DPM in an assembly shop running at 500 units per day under JIT could mean a line down situation of over 20 times per day!

Philosophically, customer selection of the SPC targets parallels the determination of tolerance spread. Don't get greedy — ask for what you really need, but then be firm about it. After all, a piece of wood in the fireplace will burn just as well at plus or minus six inches in length as it will at plus or minus 1/64 inch. Of course, this implies that the customer really understands his own needs. Study, study, study!!!

Why? Because too tight SPC targets, like too tight tolerances, promulgate poor suppliers and hurt good sources. The supplier who really tries to comply with his customer's stated requirements can overspend to achieve meaningless levels, and may drop off the customer's supplier list, while the poor source promises, promises, promises and never delivers, but eventually the customer is stuck with him because he is the only one left in the bid program.

The actual procedure would be something like this: After selection of the target dimensions, the customer or the supplier, under the customer's direction, measures a quantity of parts. Sample size is debatable. You can learn something from even one data point, but more from 30, and quite a lot from 100. Every statistician would enjoy a minimum of 100, but if the assemblies are destroyed by the measurement and they each cost $125, you may have to limit the quantity. "The more the merrier," said the statistician, but remember all were made at the same time by the same machine and tools, from the same material, even (hopefully) by the same operator. But shifts do change after eight hours, you know...

The data are accumulated and calculated for each dimension with results stated in average, standard deviations, and measures of normality. From these data and the tolerance we calculate the all-important capability ratio and location ratio, or if you prefer, Cpk/PCI.

Now if you are using the two-ratio system, find the graph appropriate to the preselected SPC target. If the intersection of the two shows a process that will produce a quality level better than the target, you have a certified process. If not, it is back to the improvement cycle. Actually, if the intersection is close to the line, on the positive side, it could be possible to accept the process but request the supplier to try to obtain a little better *centering* of the distribution to provide more comfort.

The improvement cycle may be as short as a couple of hours or as long as forever. The shorter time usually is associated with a *location ratio* problem, where a simple process adjustment will bring the distribution average sufficiently close to nominal or midpoint to pass the target test. Longer periods generally are required to shrink the width of the distribution to a usable size. In many cases, it has been found that the curve is not really too wide — it is that the data represent two, three, or many curves — which when calculated together, give the statistical appearance of excessive width. A good graphics package helps illustrate the problem. The answer, of course, is to keep the process from shifting. This is where the quality engineer must totally involve his process engineering associates to solve the difficulty.

Once in a while, it is possible to find a distribution that is just too wide, or too abnormal, or something is wrong, and it cannot be fixed. Well, you can't certify it, but the effort is not totally lost. You now know you must sort it — this may be the time to invest in automatic equipment — and you can plan your costs appropriately. Put that process on a special list in your desk drawer, however, and review it once a year. Maybe two years from now some technical advancement will make the process narrow enough to be used.

I hope you noticed there is a little high-level statistics involved in this program so far. Certification may be the first introduction to SPC for the supplier, and it would be wise not to frighten him too much. Later, when he is firmly hooked on SPC, the alphas, betas, and lambdas may flow.

After this level of attainment is obtained for all the pertinent dimensions of the piece part, it is also necessary to discuss the attribute characteristics present, but these should be somewhat easier with the process knowledge you have. While this is not a given, that is, it does not happen every time, the fact that the process is so uniformly controlled to produce stable, variable characteristics, tends to make attribute problems repeatable or at least stand still long enough to be eliminated. Now it is the supplier's design force that must be activated.

Some success has been had in quantifying attributes and turning them into variables. For example, a *perfect* piece, for a particular attribute, is assigned a score of zero. A minor defect, perhaps cosmetic, is a three. Something that slightly malfunctions or needs adjustment would be a five. If it does not work at all, it is a nine. Maybe a critical defect, defined as injurious to life, should be given a high number, like 100, to always throw out a process that produces parts that could hurt someone. Then take the scores, view them as measurements, determine the average, the sigma, plot the distribution (it will almost always be skewed toward zero and not normal), and proceed to evaluate it as before.

If agreement with the supplier has been reached on all attribute parameters, either in narrative or sample form, and if there has been no significant nonconformance in a quantity of recently evaluated lots, the attribute parameters may be considered certified. Just make sure that the supplier sets up the job each time with sufficient samples to guarantee that the process is exactly where it was when you certified it, and that statistical quality control (SQC) is in place to monitor the process during the run. Now, we want to use those $\overline{X}$ and $\overline{R}$ charts, and the p and np charts our founding fathers in quality control left us as their legacy. We want to keep a close watch — looking for trends, runs, and outliers. The customer should ascertain that his supplier can recognize a potential problem. But then again, you took care of those things during your approval evaluation, didn't you?

Conclusion

One of the pitfalls you may encounter is that the supplier's data are not adequate for the need. Either he does not measure exactly enough to create a continuous and normal distribution (the entire tolerance is contained in two measurement cells), or he only does go-no go inspection checks. There is no way around this. Statistical process control is the study of variation, so unless you have variable results, the system will not work. However, it is safe to promise the supplier that the extra effort to obtain variable information at this time will pay off handsomely in the future if, as a result, the process can be certified.

Certification is a significant step for a customer and a supplier, so spend some time with it. Start back at the beginning with the die, the mold, the basic equipment, and tools. Don't work your way back, subprocess by subprocess, or you will become frustrated. This SPC phase of the program is probably the most difficult to achieve of all the criteria, but when successful will have both customer and supplier so understanding of and comfortable with each other's processes that true partnership can be achieved.

Proprietary Components and Processing Information

The following is from a letter that described to an offshore automotive assembly location how to gain information on processing and capability information from a reluctant supplier of a "blackbox" component.

"With respect to 'blackbox' components and assemblies, we have had long discussions around them over the past years in the USA and have taken the following approach:

"A 'blackbox' component is usually specified on our drawing as must purchase from the following from supplier XYZ as their part number 1234. . . . With that as a starting point we established that what we are buying is an assembly of which we have limited knowledge, and no design control.

"Now when it comes to getting the supplier to provide process details and capability information we have a problem. As we do not control how the assembly is made nor do we usually have any manufacturing process standards specified, we have to review what we are really asking for from the supplier. What it usually comes to is that we are purchasing the following. . .'an assembly to fit a specific location with an envelope defined so it does fit the location and a set of given performance standards as to output of that assembly.'

"Now we have a starting point for our process. . .the envelope and the performance we require from the assembly. As we have a right to understand how the supplier is to provide capability on those two criteria we can ask for capability studies on the final assembly dimensions to assure fit and ongoing information on how the assembly is going to perform to the agreed upon performance standards.

"What I have done with suppliers of assemblies such as these is ask for and have received process details of how the supplier controls the final assembly process, including some statements of the controls of piece parts coming to final assembly; e.g., are the components under SPC, are they 100% inspected, or is there an audit at the assembly area to assure acceptable piece parts are provided to the assembly process. This can be some general type statements of control that they have a plan in place without giving us the details of the plan on a part by part basis. I would expect capability information on the location of and controls with respect to mounting locations and clearance dimensions of the final assembly to assure we received an assembly that was able to be mounted to our assembly.

"On the provision of capability information on the performance specifications we must insist upon information/summaries of capability to consistently meet the performance standards we are purchasing the component/assembly to meet. With most assemblies there is ongoing performance capability information being generated by the supplier as part of their test process of the assembly. For example, flow testing on fuel pumps, output at specified RPM on alternators, air pressure on air compressors at set RPMs, etc. Some suppliers provide this information in their sales literature but what we want is the capability information or studies that back up the sales information.

"In summary, concentrate efforts upon the envelope and performance that we are trying to mate to our assembly. This should give us the assurances that there is control and we are receiving products that can and will continue to meet the requirements. Let me know if you have any questions. It's very much like the way we sell. . . test benches pass them off and we provide data that show how the assembly will fit the unit the customer wants to install it into."

References

1. Cross, Robert. "Parts Per Million AOQL Sampling Plans." *Quality Progress* 17, No. 11 (November 1984): 28–30.

2. Neiswanger, William A., Jr. *Elementary Statistical Methods*. New York: Random House, 1951, p. 53.

6

Data Collection for Certification

When faced with the situation of what data should be collected for certification, a number of approaches can be used. These include process mapping, flow charting, and getting detailed process information from the suppliers. All are similar, but there are subtle differences in their best fit to various industries. You will note that this is not the normal data collection with which you may be familiar; it is rather the methods that the supplier uses to document his control of the process outputs.

The first approach is to draw a process map. A process map is a sequential flow of each step of the process. It identifies the area where control mechanisms should be placed and identifies the controllable characteristics of the process. This greatly simplifies the critical decisions that have to be made and reduces the implementation lag time of any statistical methods.

The map is a series of boxes which contain the following information: On the left side of the box, the primary raw material for that step is identified. This could be a *raw* material in the true sense of the word, at the beginning of a process, but it could be a partly finished component at a later stage. It is the primary material that is going to be changed at that step. The top of the box identifies the things that are being added to the primary material. A simple example is adding a dye to some plastic material that is going into an extruder or injection molding machine. In a later step, it could be the addition of catalysts in a chemical manufacturing operation, or the addition of side panels to a copier. The bottom of the box lists all the problems that have occurred at that step of the process as well as the frequency. When doing this for the first time it is essential to consider how much of the process must be retraced to determine this list. For most processes, a month is long enough, but for piece part processes which are not run frequently, then a longer time frame should be used. In the center of the box, the things which can be measured or monitored are listed. This can range from temperature and air pressure, to specific gravity on a chemical, or screw speed on an extruder. These items in the process will be marked to indicate that something is changing in that step of the process. These are the process variables which need to be controlled. Finally, on the right side of the box is the output of that step and a characteristic which can be measured. This identifies what is expected and how one can verify that expectation. A diagram of the step is shown in Figure 6.1.

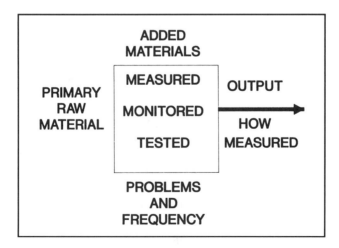

Figure 6.1   Process map showing the sequential flow of each step of the process.

The use of simple flow charting by the supplier is another option. It provides a simple pictorial map to the supplier's process using standard symbology that is used by many industrial engineers in performing their jobs. An example is shown in Figure 6.2.

The most complex methods are documented on a *Process and Control Details* sheet with capability information summarized on it. The process is broken down step by step, with detailed information summarized. Details on equipment, what characteristics are to be controlled, the methods of inspection, and capability of the process are all spelled out in finite detail. An example of this type of documentation is shown in Figure 6.3.

Now that we have a picture of the process, it is easy to identify where SPC methods should be placed in the process. It helps identify the potential problem areas in the process and what the key process parameters are for each step. The next step is to determine what characteristics are going to be charted, what type of data to use, what is the most appropriate statistical method, and what should be the sampling frequency.

The type of data can be either variables or attributes. Variables data are those that can be measured. Attributes data are discrete data which are determined as a pass/fail based on some gage or methodology. This is an important decision because it directly impacts what types of statistical methods can be used. Variables data are the preferred choice because of the variety of options that are available. This implies that attributes data are the limiting choice which is true; there are less options with these types of data. The most appropriate statistical method can range from simple frequency plots to a particular type of control chart. Variables data tend to have the most latitude in terms of use, simply because the data can be used in a wide variety of statistical techniques. Attributes data can be used in frequency charts, p, np, c, and u control charts. These charts tend to have less sensitivity in terms of detecting out-of-control conditions. The bottom line is that we want to look at these data in a manner which best describes the process.

In Chapter 4 there was some discussion on different types of t tests as well as capability indices. The collection of data for a t test is different than that of a capability study. Doing a t test implies that the process is adequate and that you want to study the process while in an operational mode. An operational mode is simply defined as what one would expect to find 90% of the time when the process is running. This is compared to a capability study where the process is set up under optimum conditions: one operator, best materials available, and the best running conditions set.

The intent of the capability study is to determine what the process is capable of as opposed to a t test which determines if the process can run to some predetermined standard. Similarly, experimental design data are collected in a different manner than for a control chart. Experimental design data are collected in a rigidly designed format that is not to be changed. Control charts use a grouping of these data in a way that can be considered reasonable. This is called *rational subgrouping*.

Supplier _____ International Stamping Co. _____ Part Name _____ Brace _____

Location _____ St. Mary's _____ Family _____ Misc. _____

Part Number(s)

3901780   Tab _____

3901781 - 3901789 _____ Inclusive _____

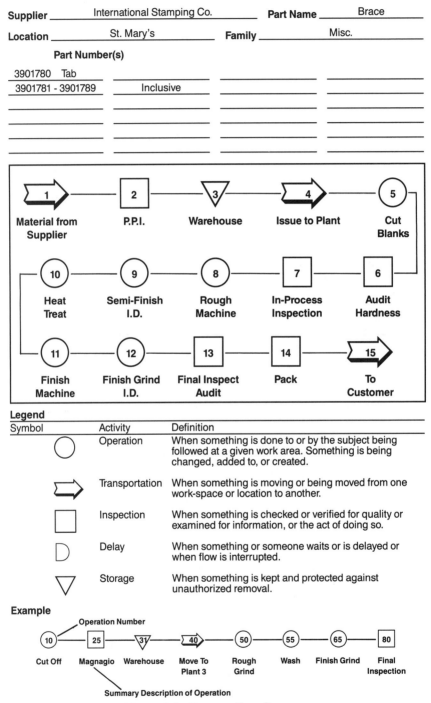

Legend

Symbol	Activity	Definition
◯	Operation	When something is done to or by the subject being followed at a given work area. Something is being changed, added to, or created.
⬌ (arrow)	Transportation	When something is moving or being moved from one work-space or location to another.
▢	Inspection	When something is checked or verified for quality or examined for information, or the act of doing so.
D	Delay	When something or someone waits or is delayed or when flow is interrupted.
▽	Storage	When something is kept and protected against unauthorized removal.

Example

Operation Number

10 — 25 — 31 — 40 — 50 — 55 — 65 — 80

Cut Off   Magnagio   Warehouse   Move To Plant 3   Rough Grind   Wash   Finish Grind   Final Inspection

Summary Description of Operation

Figure 6.2   Process flow diagram.

Part Name ___Brace___
Part Number ___3901787___
Location _____

OPER. NO.	OPERATION	EQUIPMENT	CONTROL CHARACTERISTICS	SPECIFICATION	DEPT. RESP.	FREQ. OF INSPECTION	METHOD OF INSPECTION	DATA RECORDING METHOD	DEFECT CORRECTION DEPT.	METHOD
1	Receive material from Supplier	Warehouse Trucks/Racking	Shipping Damage	Visual	Stores	Ea. Lot	Visual	Note on Pack. Slip	Purch.	Call Trucking Co.
2	Purchased Parts Inspection/	Misc. Rulers	Width, Thickness	See P.O.	Insp.	Ea. Roll	Measurement	Rec. Log		
	Raw Material	Rockwell	Hardness	I.S. Std.	Insp.	Ea. Roll	Hardness Tester	Rec. Log		
3	Store	Fork Truck	N/A	N/A	Prod. Ctrl.	N/A	N/A	N/A	Note: Mark with stores date.	
4	Issue to Plant	Fork Truck	Size of Lot	Mfg. Order	Prod. Ctrl.	Ea. Lot	Count by Operator	On Route card	Prod. Ctrl.	Reissue properly
5	Cut Blanks	Shear	Length, Width	Mfg. Order	Oper.	2/Lot	Scale/Misc.	P chart	Oper.	Adjust Equip.
6	Inprocess Insp.	—	Length, Width	Mfg. Order	Insp.	1/Shift	Scale/Misc.	N/A	Above as in 5	
7	Rough Mach.	Lucas	None	Inprocess Dwg.	Oper.	2/50	Misc.	X-R Chart	Above as in 5	
8	Semi-Fin. I.D.	Cinn.	I.D.	Inprocess Dwg.	Oper.	2/50	Bore gage	X-R Chart	Above as in 5	
9	Heat Treat	Car Bot. Fr.	Hardness	I.S. Standard	Oper.	5/50	Rockwell	None	Heat Treat	Reheat treat/scrap
10	Audit Hardness	Rockwell	Hardness	45±3	Insp.	1/25	Rockwell	c chart	See 9 above	
11	Finish Mach.	J&L	Width, Thickness	Cust. Print	Oper.	5/50	Misc., etc.	X-R Chart	Oper.	Adj. Mach./Sort
12	Finish I.D.	Landis	I.D.	Cust. Print	Oper.	5/50	Bore gage	X-R Chart	Oper.	Adj. Mach./Sort
13	Final Audit	Insp. Bench	From Print	Cust. Print	Insp.	10/50	Misc., Bore gage	Route Card	Mfg.	Sort-Rework
14	Pack	Warehouse	None	Mfg. Order	Stores	100%	Visual	Route Card	Stores	Repack
15	Ship	Our Truck	Schedule	+2 hrs. − 0 hrs.	Trans.	100%	Time Check	Note time on pack slip	Trans.	Retime Route

Figure 6.3   Process and control details.

What is this leading up to? There are some basic questions that must be answered to ensure that the data are collected correctly.

1. What are you trying to do? What is the purpose for collecting the data; a capability study, a regression analysis, a control chart, a *t* test, or whatever?
2. How are the data to be collected? Is some special equipment to be used? Is the precision and accuracy of the measurement tools adequate? If not, what are the consequences?
3. Is special training needed for the operators? Are the data so different that a special format is needed? If so, does everyone understand the instructions so that everything is done correctly? In Figure 6.4 a sample sheet for a special study shows what was done to make sure that the operators clearly understood where to take the measurements.
4. When is the study to be done? Everyone must be aware of the time frame so that all necessary arrangements, materials, training, etc., are completed by the time the study is to be done. Are the data sheets ready? Are the format and analysis decided on? Are all instructions clearly understood by all essential people?

The methods by which we choose to identify critical data in support of certification are at once both process and product dependent. We must draw on our process maps in such a manner that both supplier and customer can understand where the critical characteristics are created, the methods of control, and the capability offered by the supplier to the customer. As capability along with understanding of the supplier's process are gathered, it is possible to justify going to skip-lot inspections before certification. A return on investment of the work done begins.

PRODUCT _BRACE_   PART NO. _390/780_   DATE _2-10-90_

DEPARTMENT NO. _7310_   MACHINE _3760-B_   ORDER NO _3_

OPERATOR _J.O.B._   DWG NO. _390/787_ REV _3_   PAGE _1_ of _1_

Sampling Frequency

A _5 per pc._
B _1 per pc._
C _3 per shift_
D _3 per shift_
E _1 per lot_
F _32 per box_

Sketch

Time/Comments	A SPECIFICATION $3.00''\pm.01$	B SPECIFICATION $.350\pm.050$	C SPECIFICATION $.25\pm.005$	D SPECIFICATION $.990{+.010 \atop -.050}$	E SPECIFICATION $.70\pm.005$	F SPECIFICATION $1.255{+.000 \atop -.020}$

Figure 6.4 Inspection data sheet.

System Administration

Before you begin a certification of suppliers program, it is wise to have a detailed procedure for everyone involved to follow. Purchasing should be responsible for initial contact with the supplier and arrangements for subsequent visits. Research and development (R&D) or engineering reviews basic specifications and, along with quality assurance (QA), verifies the tolerance spreads. Quality assurance accumulates historical data and performance indices, and performs the necessary evaluations. Others join in as their skills are required. Forms for control of the program should be created, which will answer as many questions as possible.

Begin with a serious appraisal of quality costs. Although the customer probably should think of certification as a general upgrading of his supplier quality program to enable him to compete in the future, or as QA's contribution to a JIT effort, the program should hopefully have a significant payback, first in the customer's facility, later at the supplier's plant. Find out what it costs to inspect and test each material received. The industrial engineer should be able to help you. Then decide on the rules about accumulating cost savings when, through certification, you are able to remove some or all of those test dollars.

Do not assume that everyone will think as generously as you might when estimating the savings. After all, the changes you might make affect other functions' budgets. Changes will have to be made in their operations and exact numbers are required. For example, the customer may be able to avoid enough laboratory test time during a year to equal one headcount. However, because of skills required, queue lines, and division of responsibilities, it may not be possible to actually reduce one person. What can be done is to plan how the extra time can be used on other prevention-type projects, thereby creating the potential for even more cost savings. Another approach, if the business is growing, is to be capable of taking on significant additional throughput without adding people.

Usually, the actual act of certification is more than a one person function. Many people will have to live with the decision, and it may be wise to involve them in the final vote. The first stage of consent may be strictly within the quality group, but often ratification might bring in manufacturing, purchasing, material planning and control, and research and development. Requesting all these other "blessings" in the certification has its benefit. You will notice nothing in this book stating this program was foolproof. It is within the realm of possibility that even the best supplier could occasionally be considered for decertification. In this world of rapidly changing ownership, company philosophy and ambitions change. The loss or gain of one significant supplier manager could tip the scales from good to marginal or vice versa. Having all these other people concur that the risks for that one particular supplier were appropriate at the time of certification could save a lot of "I told you so's" later.

When all the planning is done, and done well, start slowly! Select a few high volume, high dollar, high quality suppliers to start. As you are going through the first few repetitions of the certification process, it helps to have cooperative sources who really want to be as successful as you do. Some will believe that the first attempt at certification should be aimed at the most difficult supplier problem in the operation. Not so! Later, when you have answered all the questions a few times, you can take on the more complex problems. It is nice to have a few success stories to build confidence in the system early in its cycle.

One of the administrative details is the question of complete or partial certification. Here is a supplier who makes six different materials for a particular customer. Five are perfect, but the newest chemical still is in the development stage — development in this case meaning there are still some "bugs" left in the process. Or perhaps the supplier has nine contracts but only three have been purchased in sufficient quantities in recent months so that data are available for correlation or capability studies. Certainly, it is necessary to capture these individual contributions and savings even if the total supplier cannot immediately change status. In some instances, certification of a few isolated high volume components might be more beneficial than the entire output of a low volume source. By all means, have a provision for partial certification of a supplier by individual product number. Partial certification is justified to facilitate cost savings.

Figure a method to notify everyone about the status of each vendor for each material or piece part. It is important that this system be accurate and responsive. Certain materials may go on and off certification quickly, depending on the supplier and the daily circumstances. Don't be reluctant to make temporary changes. It is not necessary to decertify the supplier, but even a rumor of a significant management or facility (fire, flood, etc.) change could trigger a full test of the next few lots and evaluation of the results. An uninspected bad lot of material in your approved stores is a time bomb.

Decide how, and by whom, the inspection and test data arriving from the supplier with the material will be reviewed. It should not be a cursory glance but a thoughtful analysis of the documentation. Certainly one of the points to check for is trends. It may even be necessary to computerize the data into a trend line or regression program. If the line projects over the control limit, give a call to the supplier, and ask if he is also aware of the danger. What we really are looking for is a continuation of that same stable, in-control condition that existed at the time of certification. Many customers, particularly in the piece part area, do not require that anything beyond a *Certificate of Compliance* covering base materials be submitted with the material, but they require the test data be available for their later perusal. In this case, when an audit visit is imminent, the customer incoming quality control group measures a recent lot sample, and the data are compared while the auditor is on-site at the supplier's facility.

What we really are looking for is a continuation of that same stable, in-control condition that existed at the time of certification.

As you complete a segment, either a full certification of the supplier or a partial certification of a number of materials or piece parts, be sure to register the cost figures. Set them up to reflect both one-time savings and those that will reduce costs year after year. For example, if you can eliminate a laboratory test, that cost will be reduced for every lot received this year, next year, and until you stop using the material. Don't forget to include things like inventory carrying costs (if we have better assurance the material is good, perhaps we will not have to keep four batches in abeyance), and the reduction in lots received, along with the quality costs. Every little bit helps to justify the resources that are necessary for this program.

Reward the sources that are certified! Make a "fuss" over them, make sure everybody, particularly the designers, knows who they are. A meeting with these sources should be held to explain their added responsibilities. If invited, try meeting at the supplier's plant so you can address their entire workforce. Recognition is great for motivation. Consider giving them a plaque stating they are one of your "super" suppliers. They can hang it in their reception area and attract more business, which is good because you want them to grow and prosper. And if your other suppliers hear about the meeting and plaque and complain about being left out, so much the better! Jealousy can be a powerful incentive.

Recognize what we are talking about here is conservation of best resources! All of your suppliers probably are good — or you would have replaced them by now. However, if the supplier base is to be reduced — and there are many business and quality-related reasons to do so — the customer wants his best sources to survive. Recognition by certification tends to make that happen.

Administration of this certification of suppliers program requires the handling of a thousand details to get it started and a thousand and one details to keep it going. Only a fully developed System Administration Program will keep the effort from "drowning" in its own complexity.

Self-Certification

One of the more intriguing ideas that has emerged in the area of supplier certification in the past few years is having a supplier certify himself to his customers. This process is usually a two-level process, one of commodity level certification and then overall supplier certification with the former being the predominant case.

The process of commodity certification is usually the same process that has been documented in the sections on both bulk and piece part certifications. The customer asks the supplier to perform all of his own qualifications to the products in question. This is done with an expectation of the receiving inspection history being in the DPM range. The customer continues to do receiving inspection for most of the time while the supplier is doing this qualification, usually at a high rate and then on a skip-lot basis. Document submittals of product conformance and process controls may be required by the customer during this time frame.

Juran[1] in his quality control handbook summarized the process as follows:

1. The buyer invites proposals for self-certification from prospective suppliers. The response from the supplier must include a failure prevention analysis along with the supplier's quality plan for the item.

2. *The buyer evaluates the failure prevention analysis and the quality plan submitted by the supplier.*

3. *Conclusions are drawn about supplier capability. This may require a visit to the supplier's plant. If the capability is acceptable, discussions are held with the supplier to assure that all quality requirements are understood and there is agreement on the quality plan.*

4. *The supplier starts production and sends a sample shipment along with data to document process capability. If process capability data are not available an estimate of the capability, based upon similar processes, must be submitted.*

5. *The buyer inspects the sample shipment and compares the results to the supplier quality data to determine if the supplier can be relied on to make good product conformance decisions. If the comparison is favorable and if the parts conform to specifications, the supplier is authorized to make a pilot shipment.*

6. *If the pilot shipment is acceptable, then production shipments are authorized. Data are included with each shipment.*

7. *After a number of these production shipments have been approved, the supplier becomes certified for that item. This means that the supplier is to self-certify all future shipments and keep process data on file for possible review by the buyer. Inspection by the buyer is restricted to sample inspection audits and periodic plant visits to review the supplier's quality program.*

As you can see, the process follows closely the bulk or piece part certification process. All of the production by the supplier would have to reach an agreed on acceptance level before being granted certification. This type of process is predominant in a purchasing dominated company, usually without a well-developed quality function beyond the receiving inspection functions.

This type of supplier certification, while quick and easily implemented, is of a much higher risk to the consumer than the processes outlined in the other sections, specifically Chapters 3, 4, and 5. The maturity level of both the suppliers and the product definition must be high and stable. Without a mature product it becomes difficult to establish the requirements so clearly that the supplier can develop a quality plan that is all-encompassing from the specifications provided by the customer. The benefit of such a process is that there is little need to have a quality function dedicated to working with suppliers. There is little need to change from a system that is heavily inspection-focused.

The only other situation in which this system would be of an advantage is when adding components or materials to an existing quality agreement. This is possible because of the model already established in having negotiated and concluded a certification.

Reference

1. Juran, J. M. *Juran's Quality Control Handbook*, 4th ed. New York: McGraw-Hill, 1988, pp. 15–32 and 15–33.

Problem Solving

The paradox that the supplier quality assurance (SQA) engineers face is a classic one of being held responsible for the actions and products of suppliers over which they have little control. We in management have done little to solve this dilemma for our staffs except to provide the standard tools of our trade. For example, audits, source inspections, requests for inspection results, material certifications, and other primarily reactive or historically based actions are provided. When we find our risk rising, we add inspections, more tests, and more audits instead of really looking to the product to understand it. We focus on what we can control, and in the case of bought out materials or parts, we look at our staffs and reallocate them, hoping for control by sheer activity.

Our compatriots in plant quality management have had a change in focus over the past several years. This change has come about because of the *quality circle* exposure they all received. This gives them the ability to holistically attack problems. If the problem or issue is one of increasing risk because of product design, then they can get through the crisis to the design. The question then becomes, "Why can't we do the same?"

At first glance, it seems like an impossible task to create a circle activity with a supplier because of perceived barriers. We are all familiar with these barriers; namely geography, expense, too time-consuming, and lack of a process to follow. We modestly propose a process in this chapter, but one point must be made at the outset: Without commitment by all, the process will be stillborn. This includes quality, engineering, manufacturing, sales, and purchasing of both companies. With the committed involvement of these groups, the process can proceed with assurance of success. A small reminder: The champion of the process needs to be your purchasing organization, preferably at a management level.

A definition or two is needed before we go further in this process. Producibility is usually defined in one of two ways: (1) suitable for production, or (2) capable of being produced.

Clearly, it is the second definition that drives this process. We are using this process on product that is in production, which is incapable of being produced or is being produced inconsistently for any of a variety of reasons. Problem solving is easy, e.g., we are attempting to solve technical-type issues between supplier and customer.

Producibility Process

The players and their roles.

In the supplier-customer relationship, a producibility problem solving (PPS) team needs to be cross-functional. The ideal core group for a team would consist of the following:

From the supplier:
- Sales
- Engineering
- Manufacturing (usually a line manager)
- Quality

From your plant (customer):
- Purchasing
- Engineering
- Quality (supply and plant QC)
- Manufacturing

Some of the members are obvious from the standpoint of involvement. To draw in the users of the product with the producers, it is imperative to get the attention of the managers of production from both plants. With their involvement, you will get the "push" in the process to solid conclusions that are fair and workable.

Sometimes other members should be involved, such as chemists, meteorologists, process engineers, or the floor operators from either company. This is heavily dependent on the problems to be solved. The functions drawn into the process for special skills, knowledge, or experience, could be either part-time or full-time members of the core team just listed. Again, this will be dependent on the problems we are attempting to solve. The key roles in this team are those filled by your purchasing organization and your supplier quality personnel. The purchasing organization should run the process from an administrative viewpoint. They have an overall responsibility for the management of a supply base from a cost, quality, and delivery standpoint. The purchasing organization can help formulate solutions along the way by committing short-term and long-term resources either in adjustments of customer-owned tooling, price, or schedules. During adjustments to a process, or to your specifications, all of these may be needed. Purchasing can provide for leadership in this process by determining the proper priority setting.

Your supplier quality assurance (SQA) engineer is the other key player. Usually when PPS teams are formed, it is because of the efforts or frustration of the SQA engineer. In carrying out his function of attempted control, he usually identifies issues and problems that are begging for solution. He can be what professionals in organization design/development call a change agent. That is, by providing a push for the process to start, identifying the issues to work on, and verifying the results of the changes provided, he provides a valuable reference framework. The SQA engineer becomes reflective of the success of the process. Specific roles for the players involved include:

To draw in the users of the product with the producers, it is imperative to get the attention of the managers of production from both plants.

For the supplier's staff: (usually led by sales, but the key is quality and manufacturing engineers)

- Determines process capabilities, relating to product requirements, statistically. (Cp/Cpk)
- Uses capability requirement analysis results to make improvements to processes where necessary to achieve a capability margin.
- Where improvement efforts have led to state-of-the-art processing and capability margins still cannot be achieved, they present data to the customer and request specification changes.

- Until the problem is resolved and sufficient capability margin is achieved, this may result in sorting nonconforming parts from those that meet requirements.

For the customer's engineering representatives:
- Determines end use/customer and functional needs, and assures specifications reflect those needs only, without being artificially tight or restrictive.
- Evaluates proposed specification changes in terms of their impact on product/customer needs.
- Changes specifications where appropriate and possible.
- Monitors the effect of any changes to specifications on end product in customer applications.

For the manufacturing management team member of the customer:
- Determines process capabilities relating to product requirements — statistical analysis is preferred.
- Changes processes where appropriate to achieve capability margin.
- Proposes changes to specifications.
- Monitors the impact of changes to specifications and/or supplier processes on cost, quality, delivery, productivity, and JIT manufacturing schemes.

For your purchasing representative:
- Functions as team administrator when input from either plants, supplier, or engineering requires formation of a group.
- Schedules work sessions.
- Leads work sessions.
- Documents decisions, actions, commitments, dates, etc.
- Conducts necessary follow-up, schedules special review/action sessions, etc.
- Monitors ongoing progress of teams.

For your SQA engineer in his role as a team member:
- Identifies issues and opportunities for improvement between customer and the supply base using the PPS process.
- Organizes plant support for PPS team and gets necessary support commitment.
- Educates team members to PPS techniques, if required.
- Provides necessary product/process measurement/analysis data for decision-making.
- Serves as a technical resource to businesses and suppliers on quality.

Objectives

The team, when first pulled together, needs to commit to two prime objectives:

- To pursue solutions through teamwork, by involving both the producers and the users or suppliers and customers.
- To determine the best solution for all parties, trying to achieve a win-win outcome in all issues, keeping in mind the whole relationship of cost, quality, and delivery.

Additional objectives to pursue include: clear and documented closure of each issue, proper priority setting on the problems to be solved, and not having the process become a cost-reduction effort, although this is a side benefit.

The final objective must be to gain full compatibility of the product and the specifications defining it. One way is to have a stated goal of a capability margin of 25% or a *Cp* or *Cpk* of 1.33. This should be used for each agenda item being handled by the PPS team. (Any measure of capability may be used as long as it is a well-centered, stable process indicator.)

Work Rules

The team must remain focused on the task at hand. If the objectives are kept in focus, then there need be no rules per se. In the previous sections of this chapter we have developed the roles for all the involved individual contributors in the team process. The objectives are clear and concise enough to be followed without much discussion. They don't need much philosophic discussion like some other "improvement processes" to which we've had exposure.

The only rule that we want to stress again is do not let the process become a cost reduction one. This will be tempting as you will see. We cannot overemphasize this point. It becomes imperative that the process be followed to bring product and specifications into alignment and any other benefits are just that, benefits, not objectives. However, there are some who believe that the only reason to pursue this type of process is cost control.

The team must remain focused on the task at hand.

The type of issue brought to this group will be another consideration in guiding its work. We should guide our people by stating that the process is only for problems that cannot be solved by normal change processes. This has to be carefully defined and guided through each different company on a case-by-case basis. Most of us have engineering services that can process normal requests for tolerance studies, materials changes, and some redesign of product in the daily course of events. This process is for those same issues that seem incapable of solution in that day-to-day process for whatever reason. There are always several reasons why the standard change process did not work. These reasons range from buying your competitors, to a product where design ownership is unclear, to the "Gentlemen's Agreement" atmosphere in which we have all worked for years. It is the latter that is so easily fallen into. In this situation the product definition has usually drifted along with the capability to the point where no one in either company understands what is being produced.

Progress and Measurements

Tracking progress on each issue is important. We have created a simple basic form (Figure 8.1) to list each issue to be resolved. This allows each issue to be kept visible to the whole team during review meetings. This will help keep required actions on time targets and progressing.

```
:Issue Description:_____ Date:_____ :

:_____ :

:_____ :

:_____ :

:_____ :
:Prime Responsibility: _____ :

:_____ :
:Support Required From: _____ :

:_____ :

:_____ :
: Date : Status Update              :Next Report Due:
:_____ :_____:_____ :
:_____ :_____:_____ :
:_____ :_____:_____ :
```

Figure 8.1   Tracking progress form.

In providing for measurement of results, we need to *track* the final compatibility of product versus specifications. For each issue identified, a clear consensus of changes must be processed through the respective company's engineering change systems, and production started on the changes proposed. Only when the modified specification, or component, or combination thereof is under production circumstances again, can the true results of the process be determined. The steps taken to get there (samples, capability studies, new drawings, or test pieces produced) are only predictors or supporters of the success you should experience.

The measurement system you choose should be as simple as the process. For example, how many issues or problems were identified, how many were resolved, and the benefits noted (e.g., lower scrap, less rework, and lower total cost of product)? By reporting all these types of measures in a pilot run of the process, you can sell the process in short order. This is important to start the process, but don't set up a reporting system that would pursue each issue until the product is obsolete. Stop after six months or so, as this will allow you to use those reporting resources to work more issues toward resolution. The critical single item to measure is closure. Getting closure to all items is a measure of how well the process is working. Success or failure; it's not a toss up, the only option is success.

To succeed in this process, there must be movement by both companies. Let's be honest when we as customers go into this type of process. We must admit that some of the designs we want made are not perfect. This is especially true in some of our base products that we have been making with moderate success for years. To bring back a degree of competitive advantage to some of these older products, and some new ones, you need to draw not only on your own company's expertise, but on all of those involved in the manufacturing chain. Without doing so, you lose the advantage that needs to be gained to succeed in a competitive world environment.

9

Commitment and Quality Agreements

If we agree that the purpose of certification is twofold, (1) to formally recognize the past events in that the supplier has met a set of agreed to standards with respect to quality, and (2) to set in motion an agreement that will act in a preventive manner to manage risk for the future, then we recognize the need for a contract to define how the first was done and how we will continue the performance standards that allowed certification to occur.

Certification of a supplier based on only past history without providing for the future is akin to jumping off of a ten-story building and saying to yourself, "I've fallen down before while I was walking and I didn't get hurt!" Pure historical data can sometimes be misleading or not fully understood. The only situation where historical data can be relied on is one without change. We know that all manufacturing processes have a multitude of factors that are subject to variability. No person or company would guarantee that tomorrow's factors of the manufacturing processes will be exactly the same as those measured today. In today's environment, as no one will state with absolute assurance that all is static, it becomes imperative to develop an agreement as to the ongoing methods of control of the variable factors of the production processes involved.

Commitment Agreement

Two levels of agreement should take place between customer and supplier. The first is a *commitment agreement* and the second is a full *quality agreement* or *quality contract*. The commitment agreement should come early in the relationship as it will guide the development of the partnership that is taking shape. The *quality agreement* is a much more detailed compendium of the entire set of interrelations that have been developed and will continue well into the future.

The *commitment agreement* can and should be a simple one- or two-page document that outlines the give and take of the growing partnership. In Appendix 1 there is a model of a *commitment agreement* that could be used to launch the *quality agreement* process. It provides for a review of the supplier's quality systems, the control plans used on the product, and a framework for communications and problem solving. We suggest that this type of early agreement to build a partnership be used to gain an understanding of the processes involved at an upper management level by having the commitment signed off at the officer level of both companies.

The review of this *commitment agreement* should be done separately from a survey visit or an inspection review. The commitment to work with a supplier to lead him to possible certification is important to the development of the long-term relationship. It should take place during a management meeting possibly to include a lunch paid for by the customer. Remember that both the supplier and customer are committing to a long process of joint development of a *quality agreement* of some detail over a long-term relationship. The initial *commitment agreement* should have the same status and import as the signing of a long-term commercial agreement. After all, it is how you plan to do business with the new partner in the quality context, is it not?

Commitment Meetings

One of the more pleasant but necessary parts of the certification process is the commitment meeting. Here we gather all the representatives, both customer and supplier, of all concerned functions of both organizations. Purchasing, design engineering, and quality assurance are the minimum for the customer side. Others might be materials management, quality, sales and service, and perhaps their production manager, and others in direct proportion to the distance from the site of the other party. It is not critical at which company's location the meeting takes place. The important factor is the purpose and meaning of the meeting.

This meeting should open with a historical review of the supplier's quality performance, delivery, and cost records with an emphasis on the positive nature of their track record as the reason the supplier is being considered for entry into the certification process. Then there should be a thorough review of the certification process, describing it as a long-term relationship, what resources are going to be required by both the customer and the supplier, and the support that is to be offered by the customer to help the supplier reach certification. Following this review, a discussion of the benefits that will accrue for both parties should be undertaken. Both the customer and the supplier representatives are to be made aware of the expanded value of having the supplier as a resource and partner as certification is pursued. Tell the supplier exactly how the program will affect his status for future orders and the retention of his current contracts.

Read over the *commitment agreement* together — this is to gain from all parties present the understanding that the commitment is on both sides. You are asking the supplier to indicate his willingness to be in the program. By reading the agreement you also make it clear that you, as the customer, will commit support and resources to enable the supplier to reach the stated goal of certification. If you have not explicitly done so before this time, ask the supplier's management to be present if they wish to make this type of commitment to a long-term quality relationship. Leave plenty of time for the supplier to ask questions, discuss the benefits again, and learn what he is to expect from you in support of the process.

By reading the agreement you also make it clear that you, as the customer, will commit support and resources to enable the supplier to reach the stated goal of certification.

The supplier will probably want to describe his quality control program and how he thinks it fulfills all your requirements without the need of investing in another quality program. If he has had time to do an analysis of your program he will want to discuss the changes he needs to make in his program or organization to meet your stated requirements. Either way, it is a time to be open as to where future business is headed, and that is usually as clear as "We will be awarding contracts to companies either in, or having completed, our certification program." Ask the supplier when he will be able to commit to the program if he needs additional time to assess the ramifications of what you have proposed to him.

In the commitment meeting be detailed in describing the training resources available from the customer for the supplier to complete the process of certification. But be even more clear that the program will not be forced on him; he must ask to participate. Make it clear that you as the customer will be behind him every step of the way, ready to help "push" their technology by training but that the supplier will not be dragged into unproven or uncharted areas of technology for his products.

Finally, before the meeting breaks up, make sure that a time frame and contacts for working the process have been established. Each side should know who is taking the leadership role with respect to all points in the certification process, and who is to be contacted for each type of question that will arise.

Now set aside some social time. It is imperative that the parties working this process become acquainted. Because of the long-term nature of the relationship that is being set up, it would be best to be on a first name basis. As stated, it does not matter where the meeting takes place, but given that we are establishing a product control program, a plant tour of either the customer or the supplier facilities is appropriate as a wrapup of the commitment meeting. If the meeting takes place at the customer's plant, it is imperative that the tour include the areas that show how the supplier's product will be consumed in the customer's process and the importance given to quality of product by the customer's customers.

This commitment meeting is important for setting the long-term parameters of the relationship. It sets up the relations that will either carry the program to fruition or kill it. By investing in the commitment meeting, its tone, and the customer's true commitment to supplier support, you will lay the foundation for a successful certification program.

Quality Agreements

A *quality agreement* is pulled together jointly by the supplier and customer as a means to establish the preventive or proactive measures that will provide for continuous supply of materials into the future with no defectives. It is made of clear statements of the controls that are to be ongoing around the purchase and consumption of the product. The ideal *quality agreement* will be part of the purchase contract between customer and supplier. This is usually done by reference in the purchase order to assure all parties that it is a binding and meaningful part of the relationship.

The *quality agreement* is constructed in sections relating to the administrative work in the relationship and relating to the controls to be maintained on the product. Some call these the hardware and software sections of an agreement, respectively, which seems appropriate.

The administrative sections of the agreement would include the following:

1. A summary of the results of the quality system survey that was performed on the supplier by the customer. This serves the purpose of describing the supplier's general management of quality. This could possibly also include a copy of the supplier's quality policy or manual.
2. A copy of the suggested *commitment agreement*.
3. A contact list for both parties to the agreement. It is surprising how rapidly people change functions in some companies.
4. A responsibility section that describes who is to maintain the agreement and the methods of communication desired by the partners in the agreement.
5. A sign-off page. This should include the members of the team from both the customer and the supplier who have been involved in putting the agreement together — the engineers, purchasing, quality engineers, and production members of both the producer and the consumer of the product.

The product control or hardware section of the agreement should include, at a minimum, the following:

1. A listing of what the agreement covers in engineering terms. The item names, part numbers, catalog numbers, or other proper descriptions that leaves no doubt that the product being identified is required.
2. The proposed controls or quality levels that have been agreed on for the product being supplied.
3. A statement on the methods of packaging and preservation if the product requires any special handling.
4. The product audit scheme that is to be used by both the supplier and the customer. Is the product going to be subject to receiving inspection, testing, or passed directly to the customer's processing?

A quality agreement development guide is provided in Appendix 2 with much more detail on what could be or should be included in a *quality agreement.*

It should go without saying that any agreement is like a plant's quality manual. If the document is created only to fulfill a requirement and then set on a shelf to gather dust, it is not worth writing at all. A *quality agreement* should be put on the same type of review cycle as operating procedures. That is to say, at least annually a full review of the contents of the agreement should be made to assure that it is kept current. This is more fully covered in the chapter on maintenance of the certification process (Chapter 11). But as there is much value in the *quality agreement* process you may find you have agreements with many suppliers that do not reach certification. It does help clarify the relationship even if the ultimate step of certification is not reached.

Quality agreements are beneficial to a partnership in many ways. The greatest benefit is that an agreement around quality gives the supplier clarity in what is expected of him in this relationship and it gives the customer clarity in what can be expected from the supplier as to the levels of quality being shipped. In addition, a *quality agreement* can provide a framework to break out of the old sweetheart arrangements that occurred in many companies to bypass the formal system of engineering change and product measurement at receiving inspection. These arrangements happened because it was easier to cut a deal with your customer's receiving inspection foreman than to change the blueprints to reflect the product as delivered and usually used.

A *quality agreement* also provides for formalizing the communications protocol between customer and supplier. In many cases change for product improvement or cost reduction has never happened because neither party understood who to call or contact to propose change. Finally, the process of negotiation of a *quality agreement* provides a single place to describe the process and history as to how a supplier did in fact become a certified supplier to you. This provides a model to follow for other suppliers and for you to follow with your customers if needed. The document becomes a valued part of the technical data you have on your product from cradle to grave in scope.

The sign-off of the *quality agreement* should not have any special meeting or significance. The *quality agreement,* if done in a committed partnership environment, should be reviewed and approved by the various parties to each section with agreement on the contents. There is no fanfare. That should be saved for a presentation at the time of certification. If you make *quality agreements* part of your standard supplier control program, as we have suggested, then there will be supplier-customer situations where certification is not reached. But the benefits of having a *quality agreement* are the same as if certification had been reached. It may be that the control technology is not developed yet for this supplier product so he can reach the defined quality levels for certification. One major automotive supplier we know of has more than 160 *quality agreements* but only 60 *certified suppliers.* This company has acknowledged that the efforts involved in doing agreements are well worth the return on the time and resources invested. More than 80% of the materials received on a monthly basis are not inspected because of the lower risk resulting from an understanding of the supplier's capability, which is a direct result of having worked out *quality agreements* with them.

Both the *commitment agreement* and the *quality agreement,* when done in the spirit of mutual trust and understanding, will enhance the customer-supplier relationship. To build a partnership around quality will enable both companies to become more competitive through elimination of redundant inspections and overchecks.

Postcertification Activities

The most vital part of postcertification is the *assurance phase*, the creation of a system at the supplier's facility that will continue the output of excellent quality after the supplier and product are certified. Actually, without these vital additions, the certification may not have been worth the effort. There are five major areas of concern:

1. Continuing evaluation of the equipment involved in the process is necessary. Often, production machinery is developed to go faster, not better. The variation contributed by the equipment must be understood, and any new or renovated equipment must be specified and controlled

as to variation. It must be proven to at least exhibit less variation than the previous equipment. In the case of new machines, this information may be difficult to find. Most equipment personnel are only told that the new model will go faster, or produce more material in the same time frame or with less cost. Reserve the right, in the contract if necessary, to discuss the variation issue with your fellow quality professionals at the equipment plant. Of course, when you arrive at their facility and cannot find any quality professionals, get suspicious real quick.

Tools involved in the process must be evaluated. Tools, dies, and molds have been made for many years under a set of rules developed by tool and die makers. "Cut it on the high side, in case it has to be corrected; leave some extra room for polishing; remember the wear factor." For the most part, these parameters concentrated on average, because it was thought that if the steel was cut to a tight tolerance, everything resulting would be uniform. Most of the time, the size and shape of the resulting piece part distribution was not considered — or even known. This system is no longer compatible with the quality requirements of today.

Tools must be obtained under SPC targets such as capability ratio and location ratio (or Cpk), and not accepted for use in the supplier's end product converting plant until such requirements are met. If the customer is paying for the mold, for example, he must state emphatically in the arrangement with the supplier that the customer will not write a check until such attainment is demonstrated.

They are "afraid" these worthy technicians will resent any advice about a process they believe they know so well.

2. Setup criteria for the process must be created. Once the process has been found to be acceptable and stable, it is necessary to duplicate the process each time the part is run. Even today the instructions to the setup mechanic often are "to make enough parts so you are satisfied that all are inside tolerance." Under SPC constraints, the setup is dictated by the width, shape, and central tendency of the previously approved distribution. It is necessary to instruct the setup mechanic as to the number of consecutive samples to be used for setup, the excursion limits on the sample's average, and a maximum allowable standard deviation of the setup sample results.

Some people are reluctant to give such specific instructions to the setup mechanics. They are "afraid" these worthy technicians will resent any advice about a process they believe they know so well. Experience has shown the opposite. As one mechanic stated, "I don't have time to redo the equipment ten minutes after startup. Anything that will assist me to get it set up and keep it set up is a help to me."

3. *Adequate statistical quality control methods must be implemented.* As variations of time, temperature, material components, and various other factors are added to the approved process during subsequent runs, there must be methods to identify any out-of-control condition, long before it becomes an out-of-tolerance situation and rejects are produced. The Shewhart $\overline{X}$ and R chart is a much used example of a statistical quality control method. Here it is used for its original intent, to indicate control, rather than as an accept/reject device. Others related to attributes might be p, np, and c charts. *CUMSUM* control chart is a more sophisticated approach that is gaining favor.

It must be recognized that all the statistical quality control (SQC) techniques in the world are a highway to frustration unless the SPC work to obtain a stable, controllable process is first accomplished.

4. No matter how extensive the customer's on-site audit or reevaluation programs are, there is a place for self-audits by the supplier. The surveys are best scheduled midway between customer visits. The worst time to schedule them is two days before the impending customer call, as a protective device against decertification. The responses to negative observations in that setting are usually slap-dash, quickly applied bandages that temporarily clean up the mess but don't cure the wound.

5. The customer should feel obligated to teach the supplier what he considers critical, important, and trivial. Then the supplier adds what is vital to him in his role, and that is the agenda. Two good references are the ANSI/ASQC Q90-1987 series[1] and ANSI/ASQC C1-1985[2] standards, both dealing with quality systems requirements.

Other postcertification activities concern additional products and monitoring. Are additional products from a certified supplier treated any differently than those from an approved supplier? Most experts say "yes" because, after all, you have prior knowledge that the supplier can control his processes. However, first piece part inspections are still done and demonstrations of process capability at the tooling stage are essential. In bulk material, the correlation step between laboratories is necessary because different test methods may be involved in the new material. The same attitude would prevail toward those products that could not be included in the initial certification because, at that time, there was insufficient data or experience with them. Also to be reviewed are those products that were under corrective action when the customer gave partial certification to the supplier. However, it is possible to plan

The customer should feel obligated to teach the supplier what he considers critical, important, and trivial.

less time to certify these additional products. Both the supplier and the customer know what is needed and how to achieve it. Hopefully, corrective actions applied to the original studied products have already been implemented on the second wave.

As yet, with the limited experience of American industry, the type and frequency of postcertification audits by the customer vary widely. If there is a popular choice, it is an annual visit to reevaluate systems, facilities, and product. Some customers audit product quarterly by inspection and test within their own facility, and visit the supplier semiannually. Another variation is one visit to audit the process, going line by line over the documented shop operating procedures, and a semi-yearly visit to reevaluate the worthiness of the quality system.

Certainly, the volume and dollar value of the supplier-furnished material must enter into the schedule equation. Another point to be considered is the number of new or significantly revised products the relationship has generated. Obviously, a change or expansion of facilities or workforce at the supplier is a reason to be on-site. Problems require immediate attention, not waiting a month or two for the regular visit. One supplier on the committee may be pragmatic enough to say the number of visits depends on his budget. If that is true, it becomes doubly important to pick your spots wisely and not waste money. Above all, do not conduct a "half-good" audit based on the constraints of time and dollars. Such an audit will give the supplier confidence he should not have, and dull his alertness toward potential problems.

The customer team should evaluate or audit, make its decision, then HELP! Discuss every actual or perceived weakness. The customer may find, to his surprise, that a weakness is actually a strength. Suggest, or if necessary, demand corrective action. Don't leave the supplier with a feeling he has played that old game: "I'm thinking of something. Tell me what I am thinking of."

Postcertification is a long-term activity. Don't be surprised if all the topics mentioned are not accomplished in the next ten minutes after certification. But make sure they are done in an ordered manner as the customer and supplier enjoy a long, productive relationship.

References

1. ANSI/ASQC Q90-1987 Series. *Quality Management and Quality Assurance Standards.* Milwaukee: American Society for Quality Control, 1987.

2. ANSI/ASQC C1-1985. *Specifications of General Requirements for a Quality Program.* Milwaukee: American Society for Quality Control, 1985.

11

Certification
Maintenance

Now that we have established this
special relationship, we must work
hard to maintain it. In fact, we must set
some goals on not only maintaining
the status of a certified supplier but
include the concepts of continuous
improvement. Certification and the
benefits gained from it by both customer and supplier must be held in
respect. The respect comes from the
fact that all the work done by this new
partnership can come apart as quickly
as the speed of light if a proper maintenance program is not followed.

Three facets are involved in maintaining the status of a certified supplier
program. Audits of both product and
systems along with periodic reviews
of the *quality agreement* can be

considered to cover all the bases needed. All three items should have been covered in the *quality agreement* so there is a clear understanding as to which product, process, or system is to undergo an audit or review along with who is to perform the reviews.

Product audits of those materials that were covered by the certification and have not been undergoing routine receiving inspection are required. Producers of hardware items should be subjected to an audit of critical characteristics at least on an annual basis. This would include a layout inspection and verification of the properties of the materials such as chemistry, metallurgy, etc. The layout inspection would not have to be a full bench inspection but rather an inspection that would give as rapid an answer on the supplier's continuing control as possible. Many processes used to manufacture hardware items have indicators in the product that show that dies are being maintained, or patterns are wearing out, or the preventive maintenance of a machine line is not up to par. It is those characteristics that should be inspected.

If you have established the partnership with the supplier, he will be able to help you understand those characteristics that are at risk of going out of control first. They should also be the same characteristics that he is inspecting as part of his ongoing process controls. Bulk materials manufacturers usually focus on the chemistry and a program of independent laboratory audits. These results could be adequate to demonstrate ongoing controls with an annual overcheck sample done in your own laboratory. The reason for taking a sample to your own laboratory is to maintain a correlation among all the different laboratories that could be called into service for problem resolution. In the case of either bulk or hardware it is advisable to track the annually overchecked samples into your process to assure a continued match to your subsequent processing.

Another facet of product audits is accomplished in the internal reviews of the supplier's performance history. The continuing capability of the supplier to send you conforming product can be reflected in your random receiving inspection history, processing failures inside your plant, and field failures that show up in warranty claims. All these sources of supplier performance should have been established as baseline information before certification so you have a comparative standard already established and agreed to between the supplier and yourself.

Systems audits have been the mainstay of many supplier control programs for many years. When the supplier was approved by the quality function originally it was based on a systems survey. In fact, the survey was most likely the only documented activity if the supplier was in your supply base for a long time, if there actually was a survey performed. A partnership is now established to maintain the standard of a minimum annual systems survey, based on the same criteria that were used to originally approve the supplier. What is needed is a verification that the supplier still has the same quality systems or better as when initially approved. The commitment to maintain that quality system was explicit in the original agreements but must be reviewed. The major reason for the on-site review of the quality system is to keep the close working relationship functional between the partners. If you have a supplier program that has accepted the annual surveys done by a third party such as that in Chapter 2, then you can concentrate on the history and agreement reviews needed.

The final review or audit necessary to maintain the certification is one of the agreements that has been made. If there was a formal *quality agreement*, the review is easy because all the information about the quality relationship is together. If not, there will have to be a number of internal customer reviews done before the review with the supplier. The customer's quality function will need to review with engineering, production, and purchasing the product history and changes that might have been made and not collected in one convenient place as in the *quality agreement*.

If the *quality agreement* contains process details of the supplier's control plans, they should be the focal point of the agreement reviews, because that is the heart of the agreement. The process is adequate as long as it remains in control, and the supplier can demonstrate continuing controls or even some upgrades to those controls during the annual review through statistical evidence. This is what is being purchased from the supplier. It is usually thought of in the context that you are buying the end result of the process, but that can be misleading. You are actually buying the supplier's ability to control a process that yields a product, along with the supplier's expertise in controlling that process, in an ongoing manner.

Requiring ongoing submittals of certificates of conformance or compliance to state that the product is in conformance with the contract requirements is an established pattern in some industries. If you have established a true partnership with the supplier that is dependable, and if your subsequent customers do not require them, there is no added value in continuing this practice in an ongoing manner. Rather, if a detailed *quality agreement* was established that contained a section on what records were important to be kept regarding the material or its processing, and you established that the supplier was to keep those records in a form available for review by you on an audit, then that would fulfill the needs of the ongoing certification. During the annual review of the *quality agreement* those records retained would be included in the reviews and audits.

If the quality agreement *contains process details of the supplier's control plans, they should be the focal point of the agreement reviews, because that is the heart of the agreement.*

The frequency of audits is always an issue to many organizations, because resources of people and money are always in demand. Without at least an annual visit to the supplier's site by some of the members of the original audit team, it is easy for the supplier to believe that you no longer think he is important to your program. The work required for doing product and quality systems audits along with *quality agreement* reviews should be viewed as important to the continued success of the certification program.

It is suggested that biannual visits be made, at a minimum. The *quality systems* audit should be carried out in the month before the anniversary of the granting of the certification so it can be renewed. The product reviews and reviewing the *quality agreement* should be done six months before this. It is our experience that there are always changes, modifications, or upgrades to be made in the agreement. By placing the review of the agreement not in direct alignment with the renewal of the certification, it gives all the parties involved time to document the changes and to approve them. The actual visit to the supplier at least twice a year also keeps the relationship current.

In a partnership such as certification there is the need for a visible testament that this supplier has completed your certification program. As with marriage there needs to be a symbol of the certification. Many examples of plaques, certification documents, and other symbols are evident in some publications. One major supplier had recently done a two-page spread of all the recognition awards they received in a purchasing publication. The intent was to demonstrate that they were worthy of your business, and they were proud of the fact that all these companies that had certified them had done so in a tangible manner, such as with a plaque. The recognition symbol should have space or a means for showing ongoing renewals on an annual basis. Some do this by inserts or mini-plaques that are attached to the main plaque. This is needed to show that the relationship has continued and is strong.

The initial awarding of the recognition should be a major event in the relationship with the supplier. Our experience has been that a presentation to the supplier's personnel at their plant gives the greatest impact and, if possible, should include as many of the production or shopworkers as can be accommodated. A presentation to the supplier's management at your company headquarters is nice, but has little impact at the level at which your product is made. Having a fairly senior management person from your facility make the presentation to the supplier is also recommended. The annual renewal need not be as formal but should be carried out with the respect owed to a true partner, the supplier. The recognition of both newly certified suppliers and renewals is critical to the overall continued success of the partnership that was created. When treated well, most suppliers will respond with continued improvement in product and in their part of the partnership.

12

Decertification and Recovery

T he least attractive part of certification program administration is decertification. Yes, despite all good efforts, prepare for the day when one of the star performers stumbles and falls. This error could come to the surface as a result of a periodic audit, or a problem during the manufacturing process.

The first thing to do is immediately isolate the offending material lot. Perhaps if this problem was discovered during an incoming audit, despite JIT, the material has not been used yet — everyone gets lucky once in a while. If it has been used, or partially used, a Material Review Board made up of all necessary disciplines must immediately ascertain the impact of the defective condition.

Perhaps rework will bring the assembly up to standard. Often, it requires replacement of the offending part. Unfortunately, it could require destruction and starting all over again.

An important factor here is maintaining the attitude in the customer facility. We all knew initially that supplier certification involves risk. Whatever you do, don't allow the "naysayers" to proclaim, "See, I told you it wasn't perfect. Now we have lost some money, so let's throw out the program!" All of life is a risk. Without risk no progress can be made. Recognize that if you calculated the odds correctly at the time of certification, it was a good "bet," but any bet can be lost once in a while. Just carry on with the knowledge that you should gain much more than you lose.

From here on, everything depends on the severity of the problem. If the nonconformity involved the incorrect marking of the piece part container, that is one kind of problem. The supplier must verify the contents of the box, usually in person and through records, and change the marking. The corrective action is retraining his box marker or obtaining a better method, such as a computer-driven label maker. If the problem was container damage, you may have to request retraining of all the lift truck drivers at the supplier's plant or a change in common carriers. Before you put in a claim against the trucking company, however, be sure the container was designed to withstand the trip.

If the trouble is in the piece part or the material, and it is minor, pertaining to appearance, a Material Review Board meeting needs to be called. The questions to be answered are:

1. What is to be done with the present supplier-furnished piece part or material lot, the one on which the problem was discovered? Maybe the problem is minor, and the material can be used with rework or adjustment. More than likely it will be returned, unless customer stock needs dictate inhouse sorting.

2. What is to be done with the assemblies or batches made using the previous lots, the ones accepted and used without inspection since the last audit? An analysis of line inspection results is important to determine how many defectives were caught at that stage.

If it is a major defect — the piece part or material does not function — a trip to the supplier's facility is almost impossible to avoid. Just as a police detective would proceed, every piece of evidence is assembled to determine where the defective condition began, and how many units were involved. This will enable the Material Review Board and management to react to question number two regarding the material in the field. Whether to rework all the material on-line, or to purge the warehouse, or to recall from the distribution centers depends on the accuracy of the investigation conducted.

One of the most common problems happens when the supplier's quality system does function, the difficulty is discovered, and corrective action is taken.

Part of the corrective action is to purge the lot, or batch, of defectives. Good judgment must be used in determining at what point the problem began, so the offending material can be controlled. If it is a situation where the extent of the problem cannot be quantified, then a full investigation is required.

In any case, the customer is shipped a strata of rejects. To prevent this, it is most essential that the supplier have excellent records of when every item is produced and what actions were taken in that period (sequential numbering of containers, a mechanic's log of all adjustments made, etc.). Another helpful feature if the quality "detective" can locate the area of distress, is to keep the customer's production going. "Accept boxes 1 through 47, return boxes 48 through 96, accept (after special sampling) 97 through the end of the run." Suppliers must realize that a problem which shuts down the line is viewed with much greater severity than one that only involves scrambling for position.

After all the dust has settled, after corrective action has been implemented, the next decision is about the status of the supplier. Did the problem show such a weakness in their quality system that they should be decertified or even disapproved? Remember, you thought they were pretty good at one time because you certified them, so don't let your immediate emotions or peer pressure run away with you. It is not necessary to decertify the supplier for every problem. Actually, most of the customers on the Customer-Supplier Technical Committee allow one failure before decertification — as long as immediate and successful corrective action is implemented. However, if the problem happened because of a negative change in the supplier company philosophy since certification, disqualification may be appropriate.

If the supplier is worth saving, let him earn his way back to certification. We suggest the use of multilevel continuous sampling plans as one method. For example, for a medium-severe problem, test the next four lots in a row, then one of each four next lots, one of eight, one of 16, one of 32, until the supplier is at his standard audit rate. Schilling[1] has an excellent book on the subject. Don't forget to let material management planning know that those lots are going to be held up for inspection for a while, particularly if you are working in a JIT atmosphere. The supplier must also notify the customer if the corrective action will cause delays in delivery. A more severe penalty is removal from certified status until one full year of defect-free lots have been provided to the customer. Don't try to extract "revenge" for the error. This supplier is your partner, not your adversary. Make the punishment fit the crime. It could turn a member of your "family" against you and decrease their usefulness. Again, it all depends on the severity of the defect, and the system must be flexible enough to cover all sorts of problems.

> *Don't try to extract "revenge" for the error.*

Everyone would like to believe that once the customer and supplier have worked together sufficiently to achieve certification, the problems are all behind us. And hopefully, they are. But be sure to have a procedure developed and approved if the improbable possibility happens.

A *Case Study of Decertification*

Supplier certification seems to answer many questions in today's competitive environment in the areas of lower inventory costs, JIT, improved customer/supplier relationships, just to name a few.

But as it is with any system, safeguards must be built in. When automobiles became faster, better braking became necessary. In the case of the certification process we must also, unfortunately, consider a decertification process.

Many advocates might maintain that if a certification process is properly executed there is no need to consider that something negative might occur. I would like to add that not only do you need proper execution of the process, but you must also maintain what has been accomplished and continue to improve.

Let us examine an actual case where decertification became necessary and try to provide some insight as to why.

The customer company was a larger well-known company, a leader in its particular market and in the top half of the Fortune 500 companies. The supplier company was also a leader in its speciality, although much smaller in size. The certification process was completed and the supplier was awarded a plaque and allowed to "ship to use." I have enclosed ship to use in quotes and hope that this will emphasize exactly what the user has done. The user has placed explicit trust in the supplier to do exactly what was agreed on.

Things go well for a period of time. Boy is this great. Suddenly, a problem comes up at one of the user plants. An investigation is conducted and the problem seems to be resolved. Several plants use this part and only one has a problem. So we fix what we think it is. All goes well for a shorter period of time and up pops another problem. Again we look at the part and fix it. This scenario continues until the customer says something is seriously wrong.

At this point a survey team goes to the supplier and finds enough discrepancies to advise the supplier to reestablish his basis that showed how he met the certification criteria. A resurvey in 90 days was set by both parties. This seems like it will do the job. However, in 90 days a resurvey caused the customer to decertify the supplier. The decision was based on the fact that a basic system was found to have gone into default during the 90 days! A survey done on day three of the 90 days would not have resulted in decertification.

I need not point out that this is a traumatic time for both parties. It must be handled in such a manner that the customer does not lose a supplier who was, at least at one time, considered an asset. In this particular case many things went wrong or were not correctly accomplished at the beginning. All of the following must be included in the certification process:

1. Establish a definite plan for certification. This plan should account for the steps for decertification should it become necessary.
2. Be as explicit as possible in your specifications and requirements, especially when you are purchasing a product designed by the supplier. Be sure the supplier understands it is no longer "his" design but is now "shared jointly." Not even "improvements" can be made unless approved in advance.
3. Make your drawings as complete as possible. If you accept a supplier drawing, review it carefully; make certain both sides understand the application, agree on critical characteristics, and document the controls required in detail.
4. Audit, audit, and do more auditing. Every machine must be oiled and maintained. This one is no different.
5. Keep a flow of information between both parties. The same level of enthusiasm to attain certification must be kept to maintain certification.

In the case study these five points were not managed well. It seems that we could easily blame the supplier for all that went wrong. Not so. The process of certification is a partnership process. When something goes wrong both parties must agree to correct the problems or agree to dissolve the partnership in a professional manner. In this instance the supplier was recertified and has learned a valuable lesson in being a partner to the customer.

To summarize why things went wrong would be difficult, but some of the major problems include the following:
1. Lack of understanding that the design no longer belonged to the supplier.

2. *Lack of knowledge on the part of the supplier as to what application problems were most likely to occur.*
3. *Lack of communication that resulted in a fix as a partnership. The relationship can become adversarial if not handled properly, i.e., my part is OK, but you don't know how to use it.*
4. *Phrase was used where a dimension would have been proper (i.e., angle 20 plus/minus two degrees versus 20° +/–2).*
5. *Don't always look for a fix on the part only, examine the system also or it will happen again.*

Certification is still a good tool. Decertification, however, is also an option and must be considered, in our opinion, up front. The dangers of ship to use are evident and everything must be done to prevent any exposure caused by the certification process.

There was no intent with the supplier to ship substandard product, but for whatever reason things slipped. Remember both parties must maintain an interest in doing the best possible for the partnership.

Reference

1. Schilling, Edward G. *Acceptance Sampling in Quality Control.* New York: Marcel Dekker, 1982.

13

Benefits of
Certification

N ow, after hearing the details, you can see that true certification of suppliers is not a quick fix or a cheap way out. The certification program requires a significant amount of hard work to qualify the chosen suppliers, and strong follow-up to keep the program pointed in the right direction. It is a long-term commitment for and to both the customers and suppliers and to interactions with other internal quality programs. Estimates as to the length of the certification program for a single supplier vary between three months and three years, depending on the effort expended. The length of time is also, of course, dependent on product and process.

Yet, despite all of this necessary effort, certification may represent the only way to the future. To remain competitive in the world of tomorrow, greater attainment in quality will be required, and that particularly applies to supplier-furnished material. Realize the frustration about using the sampling plans of today — they either just won't work or the cost is prohibitive. For a large lot — to give a quality level of 150 DPM, c equals 3, r equals 4, and the sample size is 28,450! As the assembly line goes faster and requires greater precision, recognize the cash impact of even a short string of defectives — shutting down the line often is measured not in hundreds but in thousands of dollars. It is obvious we must change the function and direction of incoming inspection.

To remain competitive in the world of tomorrow, greater attainment in quality will be required...

One common misapprehension of the unsophisticated is that certification and SPC will shrink all tolerances to the ±.0001 range. Certainly, the tolerance spreads of the future may decrease, but only as the mating parts and the processing machines demand. The strongest impetus of this program is still to furnish all the parts within the tolerance every time. There have been many cases where the tolerance can be opened, once the customer has developed confidence that the present spread will not be abused, or after he really figures out what is fit for use.

Another reason certification of suppliers may be the only answer to the future is JIT, just-in-time production systems, and all of its variations. In its most classic illustration, the supplier's product arrives at the customer plant within a day, or within hours, sometimes minutes, of when it is to be used on the assembly line or batch operation. No incoming inspection or test is done. If the supplier-furnished material is nonconforming, the line or process stops! At this point in some customer plants, the managerial force is immediately divided into two groups. The first group scrambles to make adjustments, or sort material, or anything to get the line going again. The other group interferes with their efforts by running up and down the aisles screaming, "I told you that supplier certification would never work. . ."

Just-in-time has as its overall goal the elimination of waste. Most all of today's inventory systems allow a week or two for incoming inspection and test, but those two weeks add nothing to the product; therefore, it is by definition wasted time. In addition, many "smart" material management people plug in another three to four weeks, just in case the product is rejected and has to be replaced, which is in some places sarcastically known as the just-in-case (JIC) system. This causes even more waste, both of storage space and money. Remember, most customers pay on arrival. Consider that if a large company paid all its supplier bills one month later, the size of that "float" and the interest it could generate if otherwise gainfully employed, could be astounding and pay for a lot of prevention. For a company that spends $60 million annually for supplier-furnished material, the interest gained would be about $450,000, and that is the type of savings that goes on year after year.

The prerequisites for installing a JIT system have been widely agreed to and include discipline, schedule stability, trust and commitment, training, transportation, and quality parts. Without the quality parts it has been agreed that the other criteria will not be able to support any level of a JIT system, by and of themselves.

A word here to those employed in the government-regulated industries, where acceptable practice demands that at least some tests be conducted on every lot received. You may never get to the "arrive at 2:15 P.M., use at 2:45 P.M." stage, but at least you can try for an "arrive on Tuesday, use on Thursday" regime. Certification still will erase the major part of the test costs, many inventory dollars, and with confidence in the supplier's product, most of the JIC type of waste.

But remember, JIT and any variation will simply not work without certified suppliers. Unless you can absolutely depend on acceptable supplier-furnished material each and virtually every time, you are better off financially with the more traditional methods of material control and manufacturing. This is also a warning about switching on the JIT schedule prematurely, before the quality function and their associates truly have the certification program in full operation.

In some companies that have had supplier certification processes for many years along with a good cost of quality measurement system, some data gathered have shown a real return on the investment of certification. One such company, in a hard goods manufacturing arena, was able to reduce its number of receiving inspectors by more than 50% in the first three years of the process. This was done while production levels remained the same and they were introducing new products. In the joint venture

> *. . . JIT and any variation will simply not work without certified suppliers.*

discussed at the end of this chapter, the real benefit was a cost avoidance of $3 million. They did not have to set up an area, equip it, staff it, train people, have the inventory wait for inspection, or suffer rejects at the rates usually found in that industry. A close look at companies that have succeeded in supplier certification shows a return on investment of between 2 to 1 up to and exceeding 10 to 1! This is more than enough in most industries to justify a purchase of new capital equipment.

Finally, the most selfish reason for QA — the desire for peace and quiet. Often the success of supplier QA is measured by noise level — how much can you suppress the hue and cry from the line related to supplier-furnished material. One of the best ways to win is to keep your best players in the game. Certification will keep your best suppliers in there pitching for you.

There is a strong movement in this hemisphere to cut down on the number of suppliers. It stems from Deming's teachings[1] and the Japanese success. Now, those that have been heavily involved in multiple sourcing would be foolish not to acknowledge that among their cadre of suppliers there are those who are good, those who are better, and those who are best. They all have met your minimum standards for approval, but some are winners and some are superstars. The worst thing that could happen for the future of quality is that when the choice is made, the *good* supplier gets the long-term contract over the *best* source based on a price difference of a quarter-cent per part. And don't gnash your teeth at purchasing. Given two approved sources and no other information, it is their obvious choice, and in line with their goals, to choose the lower cost.

Certification can solve this problem. First, try to hold off the purge of the bid list until you can determine who can be certified and who cannot. Sometimes this produces a few surprises. Don't attempt to pass a simple rule that the certified supplier always gets the contract. The first time a significant price difference shows up, you will be in for a nasty fight that no one can truly win. Instead, go with the total cost concept. Show in *hard dollars* how much less the certified source costs your company as a result of no incoming inspection, reduced inventory space, and premature payments because you can depend on his deliveries, and decreased internal and external failure costs because of consistent quality. The final equation is simple. Bid price, plus quality costs, plus inventory and delivery costs, equal total cost. This is the real cash necessary to get the piece part or material, not just to the receiving dock, but into the assembly where it can make sales dollars. Usually, the *best* company wins. It is important that the quality function be able to contribute to the conservation of their finest partners.

Schonberger[2] calls this a process of building bridges. He leads us to the same conclusions; that is, the only way to world class quality in total is by having everyone involved in the process. His diagram (Figure 13.1) shows two companies that can begin the process of certification of the supplier because all parties must be involved with both the upfront commitment we have discussed and the ongoing controls to allow certification to be maintained.

Many industries have been working with certification programs at differing levels for many years now. The best and most successful appear to be in the hard goods fields, such as automotive, some major appliances, and a limited amount of aerospace products. The electronics and pharmaceutical areas are also seeing some good results in moving to certification to support JIT inventory and manufacturing systems.

Certification appears to be the answer, but don't believe you can rush into it without a long-term management commitment and an exact plan. What has been presented in these pages is not the high-blown theory of certification, but the nuts and bolts of the process — the building block approach — as envisioned by those who are most concerned with its operation, the ASQC Customer-Supplier Technical Committee. We hope it will guide your way along the often steep and winding path to certification of suppliers.

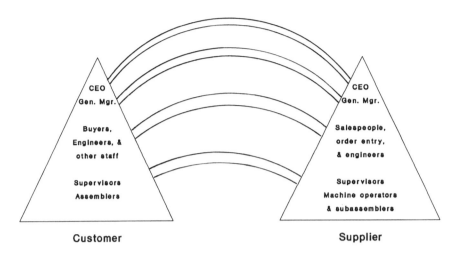

Figure 13.1   Process of building bridges (Schonberger[2]).

The JV Story

   The concepts related in this book have been proven to work in both large and small facilities. In a 1981 joint venture (JV) two large capital goods manufacturers started building a plant in North Carolina. The key concept as far as quality systems were concerned was that there were to be no inspectors. This concept was extended to procurement from suppliers with the statement that, "Receiving inspection is a redundant cost that will not be introduced into this venture." In fact, the goal was to establish and have a fully certified supply base. In 1981 there were bold statements to make; after all, this was a $350 million plant designed to produce 165,000 complex assemblies per year for the JV. The first production was due to ship from this new plant on July 1, 1983. The plant was started, successfully, with no receiving inspection. We would like to relate how it was done in summary form.

   The engineering department approvals of critical components to the design standards were started at the concept stage with extensive design validation testing. In many cases the design validations were done jointly with both the customer and the potential suppliers, doing testing with each company's engineering department with joint reviews of results and over checking the test

81

methods. This process began some three years before first production. All components used in test rigs and bench tests were inspected by both the supplier and the inspection facility at the engineering center, and the results compared and documented in records included in the testing reports.

Starting approximately 14 months before the production launch, a supplier quality assurance team was assembled at the plant site to begin the final quality approvals of the suppliers. This included many facets, all of which were done external to the plant as the plant walls were not yet complete! The initial work was to do a joint quality systems survey with engineering and the purchasing department to assure that the prototype source that engineering had been using was in fact capable of production-type quality and had the capacity and capability of supporting the startup of production.

Purchasing had embraced the concept of a limited number of suppliers including many sole sources for this plant, so this review was limited to 45 suppliers for over 1,000 part numbers needed for the first two years of production. They were also ready to sign long-term contracts with those suppliers who became approved by the joint evaluation team. The terms of some of the contracts were up to eight years, which was unheard of in this industry at that time.

The supplier quality assurance program began with the joint approval of the supplier's quality system. The program included many additional steps before the supplier became fully approved and a candidate for certification. The next step that became a requirement was to do an initial sample approval from production tooling. This sampling process was performed on components built for the JV plant's preproduction qualifications of the manufacturing and assembly equipment as it was built and qualified. These pilot runs were done approximately six months before the first production shipments, with the resulting assemblies being shipped to different sites for extended reliability tests. The components were fully inspected both in their geometric form and their physical makeup (dimensions and chemistry/metallurgical laboratory tests). The samples were selected from a production tooling run of more than 200 parts each, as the initial plant runs were more than 200 complete assemblies. The sample parts were numbered and fully inspected at both the supplier and at the laboratories of the other JV plants.

This provided correlation of measurement methods and techniques over a minimum of 32 individual parts from the 200+ part run. The inspection allowed for corrections to production tooling and processes before production launch. In addition to the inspection results, the supplier was required to do short-run capability studies on that sample run. The Cpk expected was 1.33 or better using only 70% of the drawing tolerance. If the capability was present on critical characteristics, then the tooling was paid for by purchasing. If the tooling was not capable, additional pilot runs were required before final tooling approval and buyoff.

To support the production launch, a system of source inspection by the JV's SQA engineers and source verification by the supplier was set up. This was a program of having the same critical characteristics inspected and documented on a sample basis for each subsequent manufacturing lot. The results were reviewed upon submittal for evidence of continuing control. Random samples were subjected to a third level audit program.

Based on the margins of capability demonstrated in the initial production runs and continuing demonstration of having a process in continuing control, this inspection was performed by the plant SQA engineers or the supplier. These lot inspections were always done at the supplier's facility, to limit investment in transporting materials that were not up to standard.

Included in this process was an early and significant statement of confidence in those suppliers who had demonstrated total process control early in the relationship. Those who had the controls in place were allowed to do the inspections with no independent source inspection by the JV's SQA engineers, and release the lot for shipment by telephone notification to the plant that all was OK. Each lot of material was clearly identified by tags as to the inspection that was performed, either source inspected by the JV's SQA department or source released by the supplier. Later in the process, after certification, those suppliers were given special tags that showed their status to attach to the material being shipped.

As additional subsequent lots were manufactured and no problems in assembly or the field were identified that were attributed to the supplier, the source inspection and source verification frequencies were extended by the use of a skip-lot type system.

The process of what to inspect, the inspection frequencies, and the measurement methods were all documented early in the process in a quality *agreement. This document was instrumental in allowing both parties to have a documented understanding of expectations and how they were to be fulfilled with no "surprises" for either party.*

The suppliers who demonstrated a capability margin, that is, no rejects during any inspections by the JV's SQA engineers or their own source inspections at the end of a year, were recognized as certified suppliers to this company. The certification was renewed each year, with an update to the quality agreement on the continuing improvements that were to be established in the year to come; e.g., removal of the supplier's own redundant inspections by installation of process controls, or increases to the capability margins.

At the end of three years of production a review was performed to assess the cost implications of this type of startup with no receiving inspection. The cost avoidance of not having to have an inspection area, no inspection tooling, no inspectors, no inventory that was on hold waiting inspection, including the interest paid at a time of a prime rate of 15%, were all taken into the calculation. The savings to the JV was over $3 million! This was after the costs of the extensive travel were deducted and it included a portion of the warranty costs that never occurred, because the product was launched at a more reliable level than expected.

References

1. Deming, W. Edwards. *Elementary Principles of the Statistical Control of Quality.* Tokyo: Nippon Kagaku Gijutsu Remmei, 1951.

2. Schonberger, Richard J. *World Class Manufacturing.* New York: Free Press, 1986.

Model Commitment Agreement

The certification program is designed to reduce costs and enhance delivery performance, as well as improve quality for all parties involved. Done properly, this program also improves productivity for all involved with the product, from the raw material state to final end use. Timely results require that customer and supplier work closely together to complete the necessary steps of the certification process. This process will involve several discrete projects requiring completion, some by the supplier and some by the customer. Projects are established by mutual agreement between customer and supplier.

Communication

Lines of communication will be established by the customer's supplier quality assurance (SQA) personnel and the supplier's quality department personnel. The customer's purchasing department and the supplier's sales representative will be involved in all communications as part of the total supplier-linking activity.

Mechanism

a. The customer's SQA engineer is the prime contact and coordinator for this program. The supplier will name a single prime contact for coordination purposes.

b. This program concludes with supplier certification. Requirements for certification are documented in the customer's certification guide. The supplier will be expected to commit the necessary time and resources to achieve certification. Certified suppliers are formally recognized as *preferred quality suppliers* by the customer.

c. The following are key activities or events in the certification process involving both parties:
  - A *commitment agreement* is signed by both parties (this document).
  - Both parties evaluate the supplier's quality system/program using the customer's supplier system survey process. Problems are identified and corrected.
  - The customer provides classification of characteristics with the supplier's input. Both parties then agree on the critical control characteristics.
  - The supplier provides machine capability data on measurable critical control characteristics. Problems must be resolved before progressing to the next step. In certain cases the supplier may be required to sort products for a critical control characteristic, even though capability margins exist. These are usually nonoperator controllable characteristics.
  - The supplier will provide detailed quality control plans throughout the process, using flow charting and explanatory tab sheets provided by the customer if they do not already exist in the supplier's control system.
  - In certain cases, the supplier may be required to provide outgoing product audit data on selected critical control characteristics identified in the flow charts.
  - If the supplier does not have statistical quality controls in place, the supplier will submit a step-by-step plan for implementation of SQC, showing key action steps and completion dates.
  - The customer will analyze data and parts from incoming shipments to verify that processes are stable and that controls are working.

- When defect-free lots are flowing routinely, a *quality agreement* is to be signed by both parties, and products will begin shipping from the supplier's plant to the point of use at the customer's plants without routine inspections by the customer.
- The customer will monitor the supplier's progress on implementation of the SQC plan.
- After implementation of SQC, and if product quality has continued to be good (defect-free lots), the supplier will be certified as a *preferred quality supplier.*

Problem Solving and Reporting

The supplier will document major problems requiring solutions as projects, define desired end results, and show the targeted completion dates in each case. In cases where the customer is responsible for problem solution, the customer SQA department will assure that similar records are developed and maintained. In some cases, where a number of major problems exist, problem-solving work will be done by an assigned team whose membership is comprised of representatives from both companies. The team will meet at least every other month to formally review progress until all problems are satisfactorily resolved. However, it is understood that more frequent interplant visits may be required to facilitate problem solving. Certification will not be granted until all problems are mutually resolved.

Information Exchange

The exchange of technical information will be limited to nonproprietary or nonconfidential information.

Acceptance

a. The signature of the supplier's officer that follows is confirmation of the supplier intent and willingness to participate in the customer's certification program, and commitment to achieve certification status.

b. Similarly, the signature of the customer's officer that follows is confirmation of the customer's intent and willingness to work with the supplier to complete the activities of the certification program.

Accepted and agreed to on (date) by:

_____   _____
      Supplier officer/title   Customer officer/title

Quality Agreement Development Guide

T he *quality agreement* is to be developed to contain two separate parts. Part One contains general content applicable to all plants with a supplier. Part Two contains specific content applicable to unique parts or plants. This two-part design exists to enable a *lead plant concept* to work most effectively and efficiently for the customer and suppliers. The *lead plant concept* is designed for use in a multi-plant system where suppliers ship to more than one location.

Table of Contents
of a *Quality Agreement*

Part One — General Content

Part One is designed to be filled out one time only for each supplier plant, regardless of how many plants deal with that particular supplier plant, or the variety of part families or commodities, supplied from that location. Under the *lead plant* arrangement, where one customer plant represents others, the *lead plant* SQA engineer is responsible for completing Part One.

Introduction
This section should clarify the following parts in summary manner:

1. Identification of all parties and commodities (by plant) involved in the

quality agreement.
- Supplier name and plant location.
- Customer plants and commodities.
- Which customer's plant is the *lead plant.*

2. A brief description of the *quality agreement process* and its purpose.
   - What is it?
   - How does it work?
   - Why do it?
   - Benefits?
   - How one customer plant represents all others.
   - How Part One is corporate-wide and Part Two is plant-oriented.

3. Guidelines for both parties in the *quality agreement process.*
   - Develop it jointly.
   - Will become a part of the *purchase agreement.*
   - No unilateral changes.
   - Keep it current/updated.
   - Use it during audits of systems, processes, and controls.

4. Clarify how the *quality agreement* will be kept current.
   - Both supplier and customer review continually.
   - Both review formally together.
   - Review and update at specific times.
   - Update reviews will be tailored for commodities and plants.

This section may be generally standardized from one *quality agreement* to another. However, SQA should personalize this section by recording the supplier's name as these four points are documented.

Example: The *quality agreement* will be developed jointly by customer XYZ (NY Plant) and ABC Corporation, with NY plant functioning as *lead plant* for all other customer plants.

Commitment Agreement

The purpose of the *commitment agreement* is to obtain *supplier commitment* to provide the necessary time and resources to achieve certification.

This *commitment agreement* should be needed only in a small number of our supplier relations where circumstances dictate need. It is not required in all *quality agreements.*

Approval Signatures

This section should contain the following:

1. An introductory statement indicating the joint development of the *quality agreement* and approval of its contents.

Example: This *quality agreement,* developed jointly by customer ABC company (plants) and (supplier plant) is hereby approved by both parties as an acceptable description of the details of activities to assure quality of products described herein. It is understood by both parties that this document is a requirement of the *purchase agreement.* Signatures indicate understanding of, and agreement with, the content.

2. A separate section for signatures of the customer *lead plant* SQA person and supplier representative(s) who developed the agreement.
   This section should be titled: "Developed By."

3. A separate section for approval signatures of the customer *lead plant* management.
   As a minimum, approvals should include the following:
   a. SQA manager
   b. Purchasing manager
   This section should be titled: "Customer Approval."

4. A separate section for approval signatures of the supplier management.
   As a minimum, approvals should include the following:
   a. Quality manager
   b. Plant manager
   c. Sales representative
   This section should be titled: "ABC Company Approval."

5. A separate section for approval signatures of customer *user plant* SQA.
   Each plant should be allocated adequate space and be titled by plant name.
   As a minimum, approvals should include the following for each plant location:
   a. SQA engineer
   b. SQA manager
   This section should be titled by each customer's plant name.

Responsibilities

This section should contain a summary of basic responsibilities accepted by both parties, such as, but not limited to, the following:

1. Customer will communicate all specifications and changes as a purchase order requirement.
2. Supplier will control quality totally in his plant, with no need for routine inspection by customer.
3. Supplier will ship only material manufactured to customer's official engineering documents issued through purchasing.
4. Customer approval for any supplier change to processes or materials will be required.

5. Customer will maintain an ongoing product validation system.
6. The *quality agreement* is a binding agreement on customer's specifications/requirements, and is a part of the purchase order. No separate concessions on specifications/requirements will be made outside the *quality agreement*.
7. Supplier is responsible for determining capabilities relative to customer's specifications and initiating corrective action to resolve conflicts.
8. Customer will work with the supplier to resolve conflicts between the supplier's process capabilities and specifications.
9. Supplier will describe his process sequence and controls on customer's products and show how controls will assure defect-free deliveries.

General Specifications/Requirements

This section contains a listing of those specifications or requirements which apply to all products, but not specific part number specifications/requirements. Those will be included in Part Two. Examples of what would appear here are:

1. General packaging/preservation standards.
2. Definitions of *commercially clean* where specific cleanliness specifications may not exist.
3. General service parts requirements related to visual acceptability.

Personnel Contact List

This section contains such things as:

1. Proper names and mailing address of the supplier (plant involved).
2. Names, position titles, addresses, phone numbers, telex numbers, etc., of pertinent supplier personnel involved in the *quality agreement process*.
3. Same information for specific designated quality contacts and product release representatives.
4. Names, position titles, addresses, phone numbers of pertinent customer personnel involved in the *quality agreement process*.

This section should be kept current to reflect changes in supplier or customer organizations.

Quality Systems Survey

This section is for a copy of the completed *quality systems survey.*

Product Quality Representative

This space is provided for a copy of the certificate given to the supplier person designated as the *customer product quality representative*. It is not a requirement of the *quality agreement process* to use this function. It is dependent on the maturity of the supplier's quality system.

Producibility

This section is provided to allow for documentation of:
- Any producibility problem team, if one was formed.
- A description of the issues identified and solutions agreed to by customer and supplier.

It is not a requirement of the *quality agreement process* to have a producibility problem-solving team.

Program Maintenance

This section is provided for copies of the *annual quality improvement maintenance audit*. Additionally, it can be used as space to document changes to or plans for changes in the *quality agreement*.

Part Two —
Specific Part or Plant Content

Part Two is designed for specific details related to products and to accommodate separate *user plants* who want to take advantage of the work done by a *lead plant*. It is assumed that the *lead plant* SQA engineer would already have completed the detail of Part Two for their commodities, and would not have to be duplicated if the supplied commodity is identical for all receiving locations/plants.

Part Names and Numbers

This section contains the tabulation of part numbers (drawing description) and drawing numbers. Do not include copies of tab sheets or drawings in this section. Do not list revision levels in this section.

Customer Standards List

This section contains an itemized listing of specifications and standards related to the product being sourced. Its purpose is to assure that the supplier is aware of all requirements.

During the course of the *quality agreement process*, SQA will verify that the supplier truly understands these requirements and has the capability to meet them. But first, they must all be listed. Do not include copies of the specifications in this *quality agreement*. Do not indicate revision level of specifications in this *quality agreement*.

This section should be used as a reference when SQA works with a supplier to audit the supplier's files to determine if he has all applicable blueprints and standards and that they are the most current version released by the customer.

This section should provide any special specifications or requirements related to product safety or other characteristics critical to the customer's products.

It is understood that this section will contain part names, part numbers, and all related engineering standards. In some cases it may not be appropriate to identify all part numbers. In those cases, the SQA engineer should identify commodity groups.

Service Parts Requirements

All finished products sourced by plants are also supplied to service. To prevent duplication of efforts with suppliers, plant SQA engineers should always include service parts requirements in the *quality agreement*. These conditions usually relate to part and supplier identification on the item sourced and condition of the part which may affect the customers' decision to refuse to buy it, such as handling damage, rust, poor workmanship, etc. Plant SQA should work with service SQA in all cases to identify special requirements for service parts, and assure that they become a part of the *quality agreement*.

It is recognized that there are special service only parts, many of which are low volume. It is difficult to know about all of these parts, so service SQA will handle those separately. However, if they are known, they should be included in the *quality agreement* also. The *lead plant* coordinator will do this activity on his plant's parts and all *user plant* parts in those cases where the parts are the same. Where *user plant* parts are different, each *user plant* coordinator must work with service SQA to identify service parts requirements for inclusion here.

Packaging and Preservation Requirements

This section should document and clarify all preservation and packaging requirements and reference all applicable standards. The *lead plant* SQA coordinator should assure that this is done for the *lead plant* parts. SQA (whether *lead plant* or *user plant*) should work with the supplier and appropriate customer functions to assure that incoming products are:

- Preserved for adequate shelf life with preservation materials compatible with subsequent processing.
- Preserved in such a way that added operations (such as washing, blasting, chemical stripping, etc.) are not required.
- Packed to prevent mutilation in transit, load spills, etc. In some cases, parts are prepacked in customer boxes for service. SQA should work with service and the supplier to assure that those agreements are resolved and documented in this section.
- Packaged to suit the intended next use at customer plant. This relates to package size, quantity in the box for ease of handling on assembly lines, size of package, and skid where storage is planned.

Classification of Characteristics

For the *quality agreement process* to work, the supplier must know the relative importance of all characteristics called out in customer's specifications, and his controls must be applied to achieve maximum quality assurance of the most important characteristics.

It is clearly the SQA engineer's job to assure that the supplier knows and understands relative importance of characteristics, and SQA should use the designer's input (sometimes available in various standards or on the drawings), any special conditions affecting customer plant processes, and any field failure problems (from service engineering) in determining where special emphasis is required by the supplier.

There may be certain safety-related, function-related characteristics that require 100% control or some other special level of control. These must be identified to the supplier by SQA in this section. The classification of characteristics sheet should show any special gaging requirements for particular characteristics where appropriate.

Supplier's Process and Control Data

See page 38 for a standard operation and flow process chart which is a graphic representation of the process used on the customer's product in question and a tabulation of the details of controls. *Lead plant* SQA engineers will require these to be developed for their parts for inclusion in this section. If the *user plant* parts are the same, *user plant* SQA engineers will use the same process flow charts. However, if the parts are different, *user plant* coordinators will see that flow charts are complete for their products and included in their plant's section of the *quality agreement*. Included in the tabulation are details, all keyed to the flow chart, such as the following:

- Operation number.
- Description of the operation.
- Equipment used.
- Control characteristics.
- Specification limit.
- Frequency of inspection.
- Method of inspection.
- Method of data recording.
- Department responsible for inspection.
- Corrective action method.
- Department responsible for corrective action.

The flow chart and tab sheet provide excellent reference documents for two-way communication on problems related to the process, product, control, or method throughout the life of the *quality agreement*.

Specific Gaging/Laboratory Methods

This section is provided for a description of all special gaging or methods agreed on. This section should also be used to document the maintenance and calibration of customer-owned gaging placed in the supplier's plants.

Analysis of Supplier's Capability versus Requirements

This section contains a summary analysis by SQA of the supplier's process capability relative to customer specifications. If *lead plant* and *user plants* all use the same part, there is no need to duplicate this effort, but if parts are different, from different lines or processes, each *user plant* coordinator should provide his own analysis.

Throughout the *quality agreement process*, one of the most important things the SQA engineer must do is determine how much safety margin exists between customer specification limits and the supplier's process variability (this is called *capability margin*). When suitable *capability margin* exists, supplier process capabilities are distributed normally, and centered properly, well within our specification limits. We work toward a 25% margin, or a *Cpk* of 2.00 or higher capability ratio. It is difficult to quantify capability index related to some processes, such as foundry processes; and in some cases it may not be possible to quantify capability statistically. However, the SQA engineer must still work to be assured that whatever process is used (casting, machining, forging, stamping, molding, etc.), each supplier's capability is known relative to the specifications. The SQA engineer (and the supplier's QC representative) knows the most about this capability versus specifications match, and is expected to summarize that information here. The summary should include identification of problem characteristics and corrective action commitments, target dates, who will do it, etc.

Corrective Action Procedure

Even though we're striving for no defects shipped, sooner or later a problem will happen, which may be caused by the supplier or customer, and defectives will get into the system. In each *quality agreement*, the SQA engineer should clarify the procedure for handling defective products in his plant, regardless of where they are found. This section should clarify the corrective action expectations, procedures, and agreements. It should clarify roles and responsibilities in the corrective action procedure.

Records Retention

Record or data retention is used for the purposes of audit verification and to help determine exposure when problems occur. Each *quality agreement* should document the agreement reached on data retention by the supplier.

This section should identify:

- What data are really needed.
- How long the data are to be retained.
- Who will retain the data, and where.

SQA engineers should assure that adequate records are retained for traceability in the event of quality problems, but should always guard against asking the supplier to store unnecessary records or to store records for unnecessarily long periods of time. Minimum storage time is three years, and maximum storage time is five years, unless formally specified otherwise by the customer.

Unique Conditions or Agreements

This section is provided as a place to document special information that does not fit in the sections mentioned previously, but which must be included as a part of the *quality agreement*. Examples of what might appear here are:

- Interpretations of difficult-to-quantify specifications that relate to such things as burrs, sharp edges, raised metal, etc. What is interpreted to be a burr, a sharp edge, or raised metal?
- Clarify levels of cleanliness, where specifications related to Millipore® equipment (Millipore Inc., Bedford, MA), or Coulter® Counter (American Scientific, Atlanta, GA) don't exist. Some level is required, typically referred to as commercially clean; but what does that mean?
- This section will be used to document all revisions made to the *quality agreement*. Information such as page revised and revision date will be recorded. In the event of a revision, concurrence by the supplier will be evidenced by his signature on the revised page and beside the data shown on this page.

Murphy's law says that others will crop up. If they do, include them here.

Certification Plan

When developing a *quality agreement* with a supplier and the goal is to allow the supplier's products to ship direct to the point of use in customer's plants without routine receiving inspection, the SQA engineer may determine that some important characteristics require certification by the supplier. Certification in this case means some form of statistical data taken during product inspection. If certification data are required, the SQA engineer must get agreement from the supplier on:

- Characteristics certified.
- Sample sizes or amount of data.
- Format (tally sheet, histogram, control chart).
- Who gets the data, and how?
- If it's necessary, who retains data files?

This section contains all product certification details. When completing this section, SQA should keep in mind the following:

- Certification is a cost — be selective. Don't ask for any data not really needed.
- Don't hesitate to require certification where it is truly necessary.
- Where possible, use data from inspections normally done in the process, and use the supplier's forms (control charts, frequency distributions, etc.) wherever possible.

Quality Feedback

This section is provided for describing the feedback system with respect to supplier performance. It should also provide for agreement on how the corrective action procedure performance is measured.

3

Model Quality Improvement Process

The following process is provided as a model of all the various steps in a Supplier Quality Improvement Program that can lead to certification of suppliers. It was designed with the following key concepts in mind:

1. That there was a concerted effort by a team of different functions involved in quality improvement.

2. That the process was multiplant in scope, e.g., the use of *lead plant* and *user plant* in the text, but this can be ignored if your process is single plant in nature.

3. The concept of long-term relationships has been embraced by the purchasing departments.

This process has been validated in use by a large multinational manufacturing company with operations in North and South America, the Far East, and Europe.

A Model for Supplier Quality Improvement/Certification

Essential Steps in the Quality Improvement Process

1. Understanding the process for quality improvement and making the commitment.

2. Analyzing the current state of the quality program, and correcting any deficiencies.

3. Reaching agreement on requirements and focusing QC efforts on the "vital few."

4. Determining equipment capability and achieving equipment stability, proper targeting, and capability margin.

5. Developing control plans based on characteristic criticality and equipment capability and using appropriate statistical methods.

6. Providing quality of prototype, preproduction, and production parts/materials.

7. Assembling a quality agreement, using important information obtained while working through the quality improvement process.

8. Shipping products to point of use, with sufficient proof of no-defects performance and no need for customer inspection.

9. Certifying the supplier's quality program based on full implementation of a preventive program and no-defects performance.

10. Maintaining effectiveness of the work done through continuous audit of important activities.

Step No. 1 — Preliminary Evaluation

Team Effort
- Purchasing, engineering, quality.
- Involve plant product engineering.
- Involve plant materials/delivery functions.
- Consider other businesspeople (where appropriate).

Strive for consistency in evaluation
- Use guidelines and standard forms for all suppliers.

Make permanent records
- Have typed.
- Share with other team members.
- Share with using plants.

New Supplier

Phase I (first contact)
- Review new supplier quality improvement program with supplier management.
- Give supplier copies of program summary.
- Clarify quality expectations.
- Conduct evaluations, use guidelines, and document.
- Obtain quality plan/quality manual.

Step No. 2 — Orientation and Commitment

New Supplier

Phase II (after a decision to use)
- Explain quality expectations (where required).
- Explain quality improvement process (in depth).
- Explain supplier work involved.
- Obtain signed commitment agreement.
- Explain quality systems requirements and survey process.
- Ask supplier to fill out survey form and mail.
- Arrange survey date.

Existing supplier
- Explain supplier quality improvement program.
- Explain quality improvement process.
- Explain supplier work involved.
- Clarify quality expectations.
- Explain quality systems requirements and survey process.
- Request supplier to fill out survey form and mail.
- Obtain quality plan/quality manual.
- Arrange survey date.

In either case
- Be sure the supplier understands program/process.
- Be sure the supplier is committed.
- Get the supplier involved.

- Clarify next steps.
- Get agreement on timing for next steps.

Step No. 3 — Supplier Self-Survey
- Be sure supplier understands the process.
- Be sure supplier understands questions.
- Ask supplier to call for further clarifications.
- Be sure supplier agrees to completion date.
- Where applicable, ask supplier to rate himself.
- Notify all user plants that activity is starting.

Remember. . .
- The reasons we ask suppliers to do a self-survey are:
  (1) to get suppliers actively involved
  (2) to allow suppliers to identify problems first and initiate remedial action in advance
  (3) to help us do a better/faster survey.

Step No. 4 — Survey by Customer

Overall
- Use a standardized survey process and form.
- Corporate-wide — all use same form.
- Relates to quality systems requirements.
- Provides for rating of supplier quality systems.
- Requires dialogue.
- Supports *lead-user* plant concept.
- Survey guide helps clarify questions.

Process
- Involve users — keep them informed.
- Not necessary for all to participate (*lead plant* concept).
- Explain survey process to suppliers.
- Prearrange a time for wrap up with management.
- Use the self-survey.
- Make it a team effort (leader, user, supplier).
- Be open, talk about the system/process — not people.
- Always conduct a wrap-up discussion.
- Always use a supplier representative as team member.
- Be sure supplier and you agree on findings.
- Get commitment to fix weaknesses.
- Clarify next steps.
- Agree on timing.
- Get typed copy back to supplier promptly.
- Put copy in *quality agreement*.

Step No. 5 — Name Quality Contacts and Quality Representatives

Generally. . .
- May be done at earlier meetings.
- QC manager is usually the contact. . . not always.
- Agree on communications flow.
- Quality representative
  - typically experienced floor hourly employee
  - selected by supplier — SQA approves
  - understands customer products, needs, etc.
  - customer will orient/educate representatives
  - focused on details of quality plans/agreements
  - tries to detect innocent mistakes
  - uses an audit checklist
  - works to prevent problems
  - looks after the project for QC manager
  - help make continuous improvement possible.

Remember. . .

The quality representative is a valuable team member. We should work to orient the quality representative to all the products/systems/procedures. The quality representative must know what is really important for the product, must be completely in tune with our priorities/goals, and must work on a daily basis, at the line level, to help improve the odds of always getting defect-free shipments. Keep quality representatives informed.

Product Release Checklist (example)

The following items must be accounted for by the supplier quality release representative for each lot of products. This form is to remain on file at the supplier's facility and be available for review during routine supplier audits.

(1) Purchase order requirements reviewed/satisfied   _____
(2) Part number shipped — completed the qualification process
    with customer approval   _____
(3) Part number has been shipped during the past 12 months (or
    is requalification necessary?)   _____
(4) Inspection reports, routine traveler completed satisfactorily   _____
(5) Product markings clear, legible   _____
(6) Visual inspection of parts acceptable   _____
(7) Parts received   _____
(8) Packaging adequate   _____
(9) Box containing packing slip identified   _____
(10) Special ship-to-use labels on boxes   _____
(11) All paperwork completed   _____
(12) Verification data included with the shipment   _____

(13) Special tests completed _____

(14) Added special requirements _____

(15) Problems noted _____

Step No. 6 — Specifications, Classifications, Quality Agreement

Specifications
- Be sure supplier has all specifications.
- Be sure they are the latest version.
- Help supplier understand specifications.
- Involve engineering where appropriate.
- Clarify service parts requirements.
- Identify all in the quality agreement.

Classifications of characteristics...
- SQA/supplier must agree on what's important.
- Formal classifications don't exist in many cases.
- Somebody must do it — SQA must facilitate process.
- Involve others (engineering, plants, service).
- Use a standardized process.
- Involve suppliers in the process.
- Share information with users.
- Put a copy in the *quality agreement.*

Producibility (manufacturability) problem solving
- Start problem-solving work on apparent problems.
- Involve plant product engineering.
- Involve users where appropriate.
- Initiate corporate-level team where appropriate.
- Remember, total producibility is a certification requirement.
- Require suppliers to prove producibility.

Quality agreement (see Appendix 2)
- Lead plant starts part two of quality agreement.
- Part one began with steps 1-2.
- *User plants* initiate part two activity if different.
- *Lead plant* established communication procedure with all users and other functions as needed to support process.

Step No. 7 — Process and Control Plan Description/Review

Background...
- Must know as much as possible about processes.
- Knowledge about capability critical.

- Can't do ship-to-use or certification without it.
- Flow chart is excellent problem-solving tool.
- Supplier should work to fully document his process.
- Some suppliers may refuse this information and may not become certified.

Process...
- Use standardized forms.
- Require supplier to fill out forms.
- Main interest is in finished characteristics.
- Review completed forms for technical acceptability
  - process capability versus specification conflicts
  - control method
  - measurement equipment capability
  - control frequency versus relative importance
  - control frequency versus capability.
- Use as justification to consider ship-to-use/certification.
- Share with users.
- Put copy in *quality agreement*.

Step No. 8 — Capability Potential
- Start early to learn capability potential.
- Production tooling may not be available.
- Could possibly use data from competitive parts/materials.
- Look for control chart data (ongoing proof).
- Some suppliers must be trained.
- Capability analysis is ongoing.
- Require suppliers to do the work.
- Share with users.
- Put information in *quality agreement*.
- This is a checkpoint in the process
  - may indicate future problems
  - may help you know more about risks
  - good time to enforce capability discipline.

Remember...
The long-term goal is to establish adequate capability margin to further improve odds of achieving continuous flow of defect-free parts/materials.

Step No. 9 — Evaluation of Production Samples
- Source approval is a part of the process.
- SQA must know total approval status.
- Total approval = commercial + technical + quality.
- Supplier not approved for production without SQA approval.
- Existing suppliers considered unapproved regarding ship to use or certification without a sample review.

- SQA must work closely with engineering and purchasing.
- Don't forget plant product engineering.
- Require the supplier to do much of the work.
- Don't confuse "part approval" with "supplier approval."
- Full approval comes after producibility is proven.

Step No. 10 — Agree on Gaging and Laboratory Methods/Correlation
- Can't do ship to use/certification without it.
- Assure that both use same measurement methods.
- Must agree on:
  - physical location of gages
  - who buys
  - maintenance
  - repair.
- *Lead plant* must coordinate with users.
- Supplier must assure commonality in all supplier plants.
- Should understand how well gages and laboratories correlate.

Step No. 11 — Qualification of First Production Lots
- Require the supplier to do it.
- Verify results.
- Identify all producibility issues.
- Establish formal corrective action procedure.
- Insist on process/specification compatibility.
- Don't confuse this with "supplier approval."
- Be sure these parts are from production tooling.

Step No. 12 — Proving Capability
- Require supplier to do it. SQA should verify!
- Require statistical analysis relative to requirements.
- Encourage control chart plus frequency distribution methods. Be sure methods are technically OK.
- Work for worldwide standardization.
- Must be ongoing. Don't settle for a "snapshot."
- Work to establish a reasonable capability margin.
- Verify corrective action.
- Work the producibility problem-solving process.
- Plant the seeds for continuous improvement.
- Main purpose — permit low-risk ship to use.

Remember. . .

The supplier quality improvement program is based heavily on the resolution of producibility issues and establishment of capability margin to assure long-term flow of defect-free parts/materials. Successful completion of this step will increase the probability of defect-free shipments over time.

Step No. 13 — Plan for Statistical QC/Certification
- Require a clear statement of the plan for implementing SQC methods and achieving certification.
- Should identify action items and timing.
- Relate activities to the certification requirements.
- Require progress reporting.
- Make buyers aware of plan and incorporate in supplier-customer review meetings.
- Follow-up.
- Require the supplier to do it.

Remember. . .

This is a key step in the process since we want to lead the supplier to certification. This step should be done as soon as possible.

Step No. 14 — Quality Verification
- This means inspection data.
- Don't be bashful — ask for all data needed.
- Don't ask for any data not truly needed for ship-to-use, certification, for example, avoid
  - costs information
  - storage
  - appearing bureaucratic.
- Try to use existing documents (tally sheets, frequency distributions, control charts, laboratory analysis, etc.).
- Be very specific, and cost-conscious.
- Relate verification needs to questionable capabilities, etc..
- Use the customer quality representative, where possible.
- Make data requirements relate to process needs or subsequent function of the product.
- Share information with businesses and *user plants*.
- Don't use inspection data as a crutch — engineer in the proper preventive measures. If done properly, verification data should be unnecessary.

Step No. 15 — Qualification of Manufacturing Lots
- Require the supplier to prove lot acceptability.
- No need to audit known defective lots.
- Cross check, verify supplier data.
- Look for other problems, such as gage/laboratory correlation.
- Make the supplier earn ship-to-use and certification status by proving lot acceptability.
- Feedback results promptly.
- Verify corrective action.
- Must be resolved to assure control plan is effective before ship-to-use begins.
- Be sure parts are from production tooling/processes.

- Be sure shipments are from different manufacturing lots/runs.

Remember. . .

Your customers expect defect-free parts/materials. It's especially important to make sure the supplier's capability on critical characteristics is adequate and that his control plan is effective at assuring defect-free lots. The bitter taste of poor quality will linger on long after the sweetness of meeting goals. This is a critical checkpoint.

Step No. 16 — Signing QA/Approving for Ship to Use

- SQA verifies that all system's weaknesses were corrected, that capability on critical characteristics is adequate, and the control plan yields defect-free lots. If so, the quality agreement is signed.
- Supplier is now approved for ship-to-use to begin.
- Notify *user plant* SQA engineers.

Remember. . .

The *quality agreement* should happen easily and naturally as you work with the supplier through the steps of the quality improvement process.

The QA should be viewed as a repository of important forms/documents/clarifications/plans, etc. It is a place to put/keep things. It keeps all important documents in one place. No special fanfare should be given the signing of a *quality agreement*. That should be reserved for certification.

Step No. 17 — Supplier Begins Ship-to-Use Activity

- Assure that routine receiving inspection costs are reduced.
- Develop an ongoing audit plan.
- Set up a communication procedure for audit results, include supplier, user plants, and the buyers.
- Make other plant business members aware.
- Plants should now take advantage of improved quality to realize maximum JIT benefits.

Remember. . .

If your plants are all working to implement JIT production to support JIT delivery to your customers, then the work done by SQA through this step makes JIT purchasing possible and will allow plants to achieve maximum JIT benefits. Be sure plant businesses are informed of ship-to-use activity, and be sure no supplier problems have lingered unresolved in the businesses. Also, be sure the quality cost is truly reduced in receiving inspection.

Step No. 18 — Verify Producibility/SQC Implementation

- Supplier should have resolved his producibility problems by now. Ditto for customer. SQA must verify that no producibility issues remain.

- To prepare for certification, supplier must have introduced the use of statistical QC in his plant, with special emphasis on critical characteristics. SQA must verify that progress is being made, and offer help, where appropriate.

Step No. 19 — Capability Margin/SQC Implementation/Certification Review

- Supplier presents final proof of capability margin on critical characteristics.
- SQA verifies capability and assures that the control plan is adequate for all other characteristics.
- Supplier reviews implemented SQC of critical characteristics.
- SQA verifies use of appropriate statistical methods.
- Supplier shows how all certification requirements have been met.
- SQA verifies that all certification requirements have been met.
- *Lead plant* SQA verifies that all *user plants* have completed their activity and agree with certification plans/timing.

Remember. . .

If we have done all steps well, we should have achieved initial cost, quality, and delivery benefits, and the probability of continuous flow of defect-free parts/materials should be high. The odds should be in our favor.

Requirements for Certification

1. Supplier must have been approved by supply/materials, engineering (plant and technical center), and quality (SQA and plant quality).

2. Capability must be proven statistically, with adequate capability margin, and all producibility issues resolved.

3. Statistical QC developed on customer parts/materials, with SQA approval.

4. Documented quality program developed relative to customer quality system requirements for suppliers, with SQA approval.

5. Successful completion of all steps of the quality improvement process leading to ship to use. Must have a *quality agreement* developed.

6. Successful demonstration of effective quality program/control plan through defect-free shipment performance.

Remember. . .

If the supplier provides parts/materials to more than one customer entity, all parts/materials to all entities must meet these requirements. All *user plants* must be involved.

Step No. 20 — SQA and Consumers Decide on Certification
- SQA must verify that all certification requirements have been met.
- Lead SQA engineer presents candidate supplier information to the consumers for buy in to certification.
- Arrange for recognition of supplier.

SQA now has the task of assuring that the flow of defect-free parts/materials continues. Following certification, it is essential that SQA keep in constant touch with the supplier, sufficient to prevent slippage. This is done by use of such techniques as. . .

- The quality representative concept.
- Random auditing of parts.
- Periodic auditing of the supplier's quality program.
- Review sessions with purchasing, suppliers, SQA, etc., on all objectives.
- Periodic systems audits and audits of *quality agreements.*
- Audits of agreements should include:
  – process reviews
  – part number inclusion reviews
  – contact lists
  – ongoing capability assessment.

If all steps of the quality improvement process have been completed satisfactorily, we know enough about the supplier's quality system, quality control plan, and capability to feel comfortable with direct shipment of supplier parts/materials without routine inspection by our plants and we should be confident that defect-free parts/materials will flow continuously into plants/businesses. This process has allowed SQA to contribute positively/significantly to long-term quality improvement, cost reduction, and delivery improvement. It has made JIT production in the plants/business possible by providing them with one important ingredient — a continuous flow of defect-free parts/materials. This should allow the primary flow of materials to happen day after day without interruptions caused by defective parts/materials.

How to Survey a Supplier

In conducting a supplier survey, you will be performing one of the most critical jobs a quality professional can do for his company. To the supplier, you will represent your company. Perhaps up to this time, only a single salesman from the supplier may have called on your organization. Now, virtually everyone in the supplier's plant will be watching you and judging your company by your acts and omissions. In fact, the quality surveyor may be the only person from your firm they may ever see face to face.

These survey guidelines have one purpose — to help a professional in the field of quality do the best possible survey of a supplier. Some 20 of your fellow professionals have contributed to this end. The guide begins from the point where your manager or supervisor assigns a survey task to you. It then follows through the preparation, the visit and tour, evaluation and judgment, report documentation, corrective action, follow-up, ending when you may have time to sit back and review your activities, trying to decide whether you really conducted yourself as a quality professional.

Rather than presenting what to evaluate, we will stress the *how to* aspect of surveying. We would like to make you aware of the philosophies, techniques, and realities of performing successful surveys. The methods described are applicable in virtually every industry or service, in a variety of companies, large and small, with new suppliers or old, and within your own organization.

The guidelines presented are not intended to stand alone. ANSI/ASQC C1-1985[1] *General Requirements for a Quality Program* form the basis of these survey guidelines and should be used in conjunction with any survey performed. In specialized cases, other standards may also apply, and should be used. However, all the guidelines and standards are of little use without the alert, inquiring mind that should characterize the quality professional, along with his experience, training, and knowledge. The guidance and support of the quality professional's manager/supervisor is basic to everything. Additional references include the *ANSI/ASQC Q90-94 1987 Quality Systems.*[2]

Goals of a Survey

We pluralize *goals* to stress that the survey will almost always have more than one goal. Most basic to understanding how to conduct a survey is the recognition that a survey involves interaction between two or more bodies. One body is in the discovery mode and one body is sharing information protectively.

Unlike writing reports, which may be a solitary activity, surveying always involves more than one person. At minimum, it involves you representing your company, and someone representing the supplier. Most surveys will involve many more people from at least two or more organizations.

While you may be trying to learn what quality standards an organization has, or is capable of, always remember that the supplier you are evaluating also has at least one aim: to present his organization from the best possible view, sometimes by hiding one or more defects. In conducting a survey, be mindful of your company's goal(s), which may often be dependent on the type of supplier you are evaluating. Circumstances and appropriate questions are shown in Table A4.1.

Such listings could be extended greatly. Every new survey you conduct can have its own matrix of goals. Although it may seem difficult to identify the proper goals of your company, this is much easier than trying to identify the goals of the organization you are surveying.

Not only may the supplier have a variety of goals, but the emotional interplay of the individuals must be considered. Imagine being told that your company

Circumstance	Typical Question to Be Answered by Survey
New Supplier	Can this operation provide the product quality we need?
Old Supplier	Can this operation continue giving the product quality we need?
Problem Supplier	What must be done so that this operation can give us the product quality we need?
Reformed Supplier	Has this supplier really made the improvement necessary to provide us with the product quality we need?
System Evaluation	Is this operation following all the procedures needed to give us the product quality we need?

Table A4.1   Appropriate questions to be answered depending on the type of supplier.

will be surveyed by your customers, whether they be government, wholesalers, etc. Further, try to imagine that how well you do on such a survey may determine whether your company secures a large contract, whether your company will get further orders, or how your management may view your personal performance. Confidence, pride, anxiety, caution, worry, secretiveness, apprehension — just think about the kinds of emotions that the prospect of such a survey would rouse in you.

If your counterparts in the company to be surveyed are good actors, you may never learn the supplier's real goals. Conversely, the supplier may never learn yours. If you're unsmiling by nature, you may give the impression that you're predisposed against the supplier. Then, he may rush through the survey believing that each moment spent is wasted. If you are too friendly and easy going, he may believe you are a pushover, inclined to approve him, and he may believe he doesn't need to go into any great depths about his quality system.

Such influences must be anticipated and allowed for whenever suspected. Otherwise, your company may pass by a capable source for needed materials, or may unwittingly downgrade a supplier who might be able to offer a better product.

Each survey should contain five major elements within it. These include the following:

1. *Appraise management of the current status of the program.* The audit will evaluate the capability of the program to monitor the design, production, and delivery of safe products to customers. Top management has made a commitment to a quality program and the audit appraises them of the results. It verifies that the program is being followed.

2. *Compare current performance with past performance.* If this is the first audit then comparisons can be made with other plants or with a conceptual standard. The audit can indicate trends and thereby show the effect of changes in the program, people, or products.

3. *Locate areas of strengths and weaknesses.* Potential problem areas will be identified which pinpoint the improvement possibilities that will, in the long run, lead to a safer product or a more marketable product at less cost. Corrective action is initiated when deficiencies are found.

4. *Generate an awareness of and an enthusiasm for the program.* The human resources of a company are its most cherished asset. An audit that leaves the auditees with a negative feeling has missed the target. The educational and motivational aspects of the audit should be emphasized because an effective audit can change the organization's behavior toward quality.

5. *Cost effectiveness.* The cost of the audit and, for that matter, the entire program must be balanced by a reduction in the risk of recall and litigation expenses. In addition, a better product improves customer goodwill and enhances future sales, which leads to further improvement in the cost picture. By adhering to these five objectives, the audit will become an effective instrument for management decision making.

An additional but usually unstated goal is one of team building. Although the idea of an audit may appear to be unsettling, the quality audit can be a helpful tool in engineering the teamwork that results in high quality. This should be one of the results of a well-designed and implemented audit program.

The audit of various departments and divisions reinforces their common purpose and goals, which are to satisfy customer needs with regard to the product or service supplied.

The audit provides an opportunity for exchange of ideas and methods through discussions between auditors and auditees. This exchange of information as well as an evaluation of performance on a common basis enables the audit to bring various functions into contact with the rest of the company and customers.

Preparation for the Survey

When preparing for a supplier survey, you will naturally want to gather as many facts and figures about the supplier as possible. In doing this, it's important to keep in mind your company's goals, and any existing history of relationships between the supplier and your company.

If a current supplier is to be surveyed, available documentation in your company files should be reviewed. These could include receiving inspection reports, purchasing agent's periodic reports, records of corrective action, delivery records, outstanding contract quantities, product specifications, etc.

If your company has had problems with the supplier, you may want to contact the designers, purchasers, inspectors, and production people in your plant for their opinions. However, you must be careful and realize that some of these people may themselves be associated with the causes of the problems.

For new or potential suppliers, your purchasing agent's and advanced design engineer's reports, if they have visited the supplier, are essential. Don't ignore information you might get from the supplier's annual reports, from Dunn & Bradstreet, or from your professional colleagues in other companies. If you know the names of the supplier's QC personnel, glance at the author index of various quality and other technical journals. Any articles published under their names may give you an insight into the supplier's quality philosophy. Similar information on other companies in the same business is also helpful, particularly if data on the company to be surveyed are difficult to find.

However, it must always be kept in mind that preliminary information should never be used to prejudge a supplier. The preliminary information is only a guide to what to look for with a supplier.

When approaching an industry segment or supplier with whom you have never done business, be careful of the sophistication level you expect. Always keep in mind your company's needs and the supplier's ability to meet those particular needs. Someone in the drug industry evaluating a plastics company for its capability to produce trays might be horrified at not finding a quality control manager, department, or inspector. But the company may be fully capable of producing the right goods at the right price. In such situations, the true quality professional will try to become as knowledgeable as possible about what is current practice in this, at least to him, strange industry, and to always keep in mind just what his company requires from each type of supplier.

A final note on preparation — try, whenever possible, to document both positive and negative information. Receiving inspection may claim that a supplier is unacceptable. Yet a fuller examination of the records may show that internal problems are the real problem. However, an "A-OK" report may really mean that the supplier's shipments came in so late that incoming inspection was dropped in favor of on-line culling to keep production going. These are supplier problems induced by the supplier and capable of internal correction by the supplier.

Team Organization

More often than not, the quality professional conducting the survey will have little to do with the makeup, selection, and organization of the team. The survey team may consist of only the quality professional who will visit the supplier for a few hours, or several professionals from varied disciplines who may stay a week. Whatever the scope of the survey, whether one person or several, remember that you are part of a team, and that you represent the company.

Even one-person surveys by quality professionals may bare information on labor negotiations, procurement policy, new design concepts, process capabilities, or security for report to concerned departments, such as the personnel department, purchasing, development, engineering, or shipping. When favorable, such information is usually pointed out with pride by the supplier, and he would be surprised if your report did not mention them.

The effect on concerned departments in your company is reasonably predictable: Your personnel department is gratified that labor negotiations are progressing; research and development may want to follow-up new design concepts; the engineering department may feel safer if it believes that production people are in charge of the process; and your shipping department may draw comfort from the impression that the safety of the product in transit is assured.

The moral is: *Do not stick blindly to checklists.* Keep your ears and mind open to receive useful information of any kind. This is easier with a team approach, because rarely are two people on a team specialists in the same field. A forewarned quality professional will approach the survey with a receptive attitude.

The ideal team would encompass the areas of purchasing, design, and use. By this ideal a team would be made up of a buyer, engineering, and a member of the production function who consumes the product. A quality representative is usually the glue to a team because he has the standardized checklists that allow the different functions to assess what they see during the survey.

Often, on multimember teams, purchasing will participate. Sometimes, with purchasing present, the impression may arise that purchasing should head the team in the belief that they must control intimate vendor contracts. Heading the survey team by someone from purchasing is not absolutely essential, unless a considered company policy so dictates. Whoever heads the team must consider findings of others who are usually more expert in areas other than the team leader's speciality.

An organization meeting must be held after the survey team is picked to set strategy and outline responsibilities. Such decisions should be made well in advance of the team's visit to the supplier. Do not schedule this important meeting for the airport waiting room, or en route, or at the hotel the night before the meeting. Someone may miss the plane, you may not be seated together, and you may be able to meet the suppliers only a few minutes before your survey is about to begin.

Meetings to organize the survey team should take place well in advance of the actual survey. Your company goals should be clearly recognized and discussed openly. Each team member should be assigned his area of responsibilities, and his particular objectives. Information about the supplier, of potential interest, should be made available.

If the team includes more than one member with a given speciality, specific responsibilities should be clearly assigned so that the team does not falter. It is also important at this time to agree on who will be the team leader, to be responsible for the coordination and administration of the survey.

If the necessary preliminary meetings are held early enough, it is usually possible to identify the need for extra personnel, information, or support, so that they may be supplied by request to your management.

It may be decided that you need a facilities engineer, more product information, or a better analysis of the field complaints on the supplier's merchandise. If the upcoming survey is particularly important and the team roster is supposed to include an inexperienced person, and remember everyone has to make a start sometime, it may be possible to put the learner on another team for training-by-doing, or to otherwise give him preliminary instruction.

Although it may seem perfectly obvious to you, many surveys run into problems by not checking:

- The current address and phone number of the supplier.
- The name of the host individual you will contact.
- The correct date for the survey.
- That before leaving for the survey, the supplier is ready for the survey.

Use of Quantification in the Evaluation Format

The end result of all surveys should be a decision. Ideally, the decision should be a clear-cut acceptance or rejection. With complex undertakings such as a manufacturing process, this may not always be feasible. An area of indecision, large or small, may remain and must be considered in any final recommendation of the survey team.

To minimize such a gray area, a survey team must clarify and formalize its approach to information collection and quantification. Many different tactics can be adopted as long as *the major requirements for an adequate system* are evaluated equally in each facility you review.

Valid and acceptable measurements are any that are reproducible within limits which do not compromise the usefulness of the initial quantity evaluated. A supplier survey is one form of measurement. Thus, all methodology that ensures accuracy, impartiality, and repeatability of physical measurements applies to supplier surveys of performance measurements. Numeric, alphabetic, or other regularly sequenced scores must be used if you want to make valid judgments. The most direct way of checking repeatability of a survey is to quantify the measurements.

Statistics are available to show the interrelationships between cause and effect in a random system of events. The fundamental model for any production process is just that, a process whose variability is determined by a system of events that occur at random. Some manufacturing processes do not conform exactly to this model, but the mathematics can still be adapted to draw useful conclusions.

The main reason for a survey is to estimate or, preferably, measure the extent to which the supplier operates under a planned quality system. Never forget that the reason you are there is that your company needs the type of products the supplier can produce. If the supplier has carefully quantified his product mechanics, provided a quality measuring system, and an adequate control and corrective network, the survey will be significantly more accurate. If the survey team has to provide or extemporize means of such quantification, the results may not be as accurate or predictable, especially when they are reviewed by another individual remote from the site of the survey.

Gather all information available to make decisions. Have your supplier's staff fill out a presurvey evaluation or audit form before you visit him. This evaluation form will inform him as to what kind of information you wish to obtain. Also, you will be able to judge how well your supplier reacts to communication from outside his company. The physical survey should follow soon after receiving the completed evaluation form from your supplier.

Your survey will be used by people who have not visited the plant under review or who may not know you personally. Be careful to describe all quantification methods, the rating scales used, and see to it that the report is comprehensible without your personal explanation or amplification of the results.

Your survey will be used to compare competing sources of services or materials essential to your company's production. The award of contracts will likely depend on information contained in it. The survey must be straightforward and intelligible, capable of supplying figures for cost and other computations that must be made during the selection process.

Lastly, everyone has a personal error level, although not everyone is normally aware of his own error tendency. This is a product of previous activity, experience, and lifestyle. The format of any survey must seek to minimize variability from this cause.

Opening Conference

The first order of business when you arrive at the supplier's plant is the opening conference. It's get acquainted time! Explain exactly why you are there, what you are trying to accomplish and, in a general way, the sort of results you expect.

If your purchasing agent is a member of your team and has met the people from the supplier, let him introduce you. Have him emphasize the importance of your evaluation and its effect on future business with the supplier.

For the supplier, the meeting should be attended by his quality manager, sales manager, head of the engineering department, other operating managers, the executive over all these groups, and his boss, if possible. It is essential that all levels of supplier management understand the scope and purpose of the evaluation survey. If you have had the supplier fill out a presurvey evaluation report that addresses all the major areas you will be auditing, it should become obvious which functions the supplier should have at the opening conference.

The explanation of your purpose should help calm the supplier's management, especially if they have not been surveyed often or if, unhappily, they have recently been visited by an inept surveyor! It is unbelievable what some people imagine is going to happen, despite what they were told when you first arranged your visit. Reactions may range from, "They're just here to get out of their offices!" "This will be a military type white glove inspection!" "Heck, it's just another Mickey Mouse program!" to a defiant, "We can teach them a few things." Since the truth lies, as usual, somewhere in between, it is important that a correct perspective be established.

The opening conference is also the time to establish your credentials. False modesty is as out of place as a "snow job." Stick to the facts. It is not wrong to impress the supply management with what you know. Avoid bragging or exaggeration, because you will surely come out looking like a fool. Explain firmly that you are a professional in the field of quality, and that you have had training and experience in evaluation, if such is really the case. If you are entitled to some special distinction or designation, that is, if you are an ASQC certified quality engineer, or certified quality auditor, then tell them; this is not just mere name-dropping. The surveyor should briefly discuss his role in his own company, his expertise in the supplier's field if he has any, without lame excuses if he lacks such expertise, and his understanding of components, materials, or services for which the supplier is being considered.

Handle the establishment of credentials in a calm, confident way. If you have any fears about this part of your visit, try a bit of role-playing with your peer group before the trip — rehearse your act! And, above all, be honest and friendly!

Everything said up to now about the opening conference is to assure that the supplier is comfortable with you. If he is at ease — if he knows that you are knowledgeable enough to give him a fair and sound evaluation — he is likely to be open, cooperative, and not at all defensive. But if he does not know where you stand, he will ponder the meaning of every question.

Of course, if the supplier has shaky quality, explanation of your credentials may tend to make him apprehensive. If you sense this, remind him that your team has come only to see the present situation in his plant. Tell him you are eager to indicate what kind of changes may put him in the ranks of a potential supplier. Your sincere reassurance may well convince him that he stands to benefit from your survey, and you may gain cooperation.

The next step is the supplier's. You should ask one of the executives present for a general description of the company, when founded, how many plants, people, etc., just to update or verify your previous research on the company. Ask the quality manager to describe his quality system — the reporting level of the personnel with whom he works. He should briefly discuss the handling of design information, the manufacturing and test equipment, the nature of the inspections and tests, and the documentation that supports the whole program.

At this point, the survey team is trying to get a general feel for the quality program — how it works, how it fits together, what are the checkpoints — in brief, trying to understand what they will be viewing shortly on the plant tour. This is not yet the time to ask for detailed explanations, and certainly not the place to try to make a judgment on the workability of any facet of the quality program.

The opening conference is, however, a good time to make at least a preliminary judgment on management attitude toward quality. If the supplier's personnel are serious, yet excited, about their efforts to achieve high quality, you can do a lot with that supplier, even if he hasn't got it all together at the moment. If the company executives appear to look on their quality system as a necessary evil, a required but unwelcome overhead, tread most carefully and alertly.

The most significant features or critical characteristics of the component, material, or service to be provided should be mentioned in the opening conference. This will give the supplier's quality manager a chance to explain in fuller detail and depth how his system seeks to control such particular facets of requirements.

What if, at the opening conference, the company president quietly admits that he lacks a formal quality control organization? This takes careful thought and handling. The evaluator must ferret out who controls the quality of the product, no matter what their actual titles may be. The evaluator must unravel the quality responsibilities granted to each part of the manufacturing and engineering functions. The surveyor must see the operation in action.

Only then can he judge if the lack of a formal quality organization so weakens the assurance of quality as to disqualify the company. Some, although few, companies that have no QC group have as good a quality system as could be expected in their particular industry. Sometimes, especially in smaller companies, the top boss is quite quality-conscious and exacts a high quality product.

What else can you do at an opening conference? At some time during the opening conference the survey team should ask about significant problems the supplier has identified and is in the process of correcting. The opening conference is also a good time for the survey team to brief the supplier on the intended use of the product and to discuss design adequacy, limitations, etc. The good evaluator takes plenty of notes — better to put down more than you need than miss important tidbits. Most of the time, there will be so many facts fired at you that it will be impossible to evaluate their significance at the moment.

Often, such evaluation must wait until you are writing your report. If the supplier's group is not inhibited by one, a tape recorder may be helpful.

There is a fringe benefit from trying to take written notes. The obvious effort of trying to keep up in writing with the spoken words tends to keep the pace more manageable. Both sides have more time to formulate questions and to reflect a bit on their responses. After you have enough notes, it's time for the next step in the survey: the plant tour.

Handle the opening conference carefully. If it is mismanaged, it can spoil the whole evaluation. Carried off skillfully, it can make a valid and accurate survey much easier.

What to Look for in the Quality Program

A major concern of your survey team is how to look at the quality program. This is important because few quality programs are exactly alike. Programs differ, and each must be considered in the context of its environment, top management policies, and employee personalities.

Each program should include coverage of the basic elements that apply to their type of industry and process. The basic elements from ANSI/ASQC Q94 are listed in Table A4.2 as a starting point and will not be dealt with in detail. Additionally, product reliability development and quality information feedback are important elements to be considered. There are many good checklists being developed around the Q90 series standards that can be used as a starting point if you do not as yet have them.

The objective of your survey is to see if the combination of quality system and plant facility can consistently assure that the purchased product meets specification requirements. Your main task in the survey is to conduct an evaluation of the quality program, not to dictate specific system changes.

To be effective, a quality program must be supported by top management, even though it is carried out at lower levels. A top management quality policy statement for guidance and authority to initiate and operate the quality plan should be established. The quality statement reflects a company's dedication to supply product or service as stated. Because of its implications to quality, you need to become familiar with the policy.

It is important that the quality function be separated from the manufacturing function, and either report to top management, or to a level that has direct access to top management.

The combination of the quality system and plant facility may be viewed from the aspect of the system or the aspect of the process. One or the other, or both, may be evaluated on the same visit, but not necessarily by the same member of the survey team.

Several basic considerations should be noted as the survey team considers the quality system. The plan should concentrate on defect prevention and should provide best control where personnel capabilities are weakest or lacking.

Paragraph or subsection number in Q94	Title
4	Management responsibility
5	Quality system principles
5.4	Auditing the quality system (internal)
6	Economics — quality-related cost considerations
7	Quality in marketing (contract review)
8	Quality in specification and design (design control)
9	Quality in procurement (purchasing)
10	Quality in production (process control)
11	Control of production
11.2	Material control and traceability (product identification and traceability)
11.7	Control of verification status (inspection and test status)
12	Product verification (inspection and testing)
13	Control of measuring and test equipment (inspection, measuring, and test equipment)
14	Nonconformity (control of nonconforming product)
15	Corrective action
16	Handling and postproduction functions (handling, storage, packaging, and delivery)
16.2	After-sales servicing
17	Quality documentation and records (document control)
17.3	Quality records
18	Personnel (training)
19	Product safety and liability
20	Use of statistical methods (statistical techniques)

Table A4.2   Basic elements from ANSI/ASQC Q94-1987 series.[2]

The plan must define responsibility for each of its elements. It should also provide for planning and documentation of information feedback to measure the effectiveness of the plan adequately. This should include a breakdown of quality costs in the broad sense.

When you evaluate process controls, you should be aware whether control elements are included in the operator's written process instructions. Are the customer's minimum requirements for specification conformance a part of process control? Assuming you observe a satisfactory control that identifies, evaluates, and segregates nonconforming products, does the plan provide for action to prevent recurrence of the defects? You should end your process evaluation by assuring yourself that sufficient documentation is kept to verify the effectiveness of the program.

How to Gain the Most from a Plant Tour Including Proprietary Data and Areas

The decision to visit a plant usually results from the realization that required information or assurance of compliance with contractual agreements can only be obtained by a visit to the plant. As suggested by foregoing parts of this publication, you will have outlined an agenda or plan well before your visit, to make a plant tour as helpful as possible.

As your tour progresses, observe the corners of various rooms and areas to see if the floor has been recently swept or washed. If cleaning or washing of such areas looks like a sometime thing, beware! Your hosts may consider your visit special and may be taking extraordinary steps to impress you.

Check all instrumentation and/or testing equipment for noticeable patterns of dust marks, particularly in areas where there should be minimal dust if the instruments or equipment are used regularly. If any of the instruments or equipment have covers, check to see if they are clean all over. If not, this may indicate that the instruments or equipment are not used much.

Try to look at some or all of the quality control procedure manuals, such as would be used by plant inspectors/monitors/auditors. Fingerprints, smudges, stains, frayed edges, and turned pages might mean that the procedures were in use at the plant. It may mean, however, that the procedures were not updated often. Look for dates of revision, particularly if given in open figures. You might casually inquire from plant personnel who should be using the procedures if they have ever seen or heard of the quality control manual.

Try to determine how samples are chosen for inspection, where they are taken, and at what intervals. What you observe in this respect will tell you if quality inspection is well-planned and executed or whether it is haphazard afterthought. With many plants and products, look for retained samples and how they are managed. Systematic operation of a retained sample library will tell you that top management is really quality conscious or, having had a bad quality experience in the past, they are hoping to learn from problems and how to avoid them.

If you're going to discuss proprietary information, or visit areas where proprietary products or processes are open to your view, your team should get competent legal instruction *BEFORE* your visit. Determine with your host which specific areas are considered proprietary, trying to distinguish between those that are truly proprietary and those that represent novel company practices that cannot be legally protected.

Don't sign secrecy agreements until your attorney has scrutinized their contents, has discussed the extent of your obligations under them, and has given his approval. Hold to the essential few the members of your team who may involve themselves with access to proprietary data.

Naturally, under no conditions should you disclose proprietary data in violation of a signed agreement. Your team should interest itself only in those areas or processes that can truly affect your product of interest.

Evaluation of a Record System

Before you can evaluate a record system, you must define management and contractual requirements. In most procurements, contractual requirements demand that the supplier establish an inspection system. A valid inspection system requires not only documentary evidence of the quality status of the product, but must also include all facets that contribute to quality, such as inspection records, test data sheets, raw material certification, heat-treating records, calibration data, plating records, X-rays, etc.

Perhaps the most effective way to evaluate a record system at the inspection level is to select a lot/part/assembly and trace it back to the raw material state. Choose a specimen that is not too old, so the supplier can't duck behind, "This is before my time," or so new that, "It isn't completed." Pick a sample within the oldest time frame acceptable to the supplier in which time frame excuses for nonconformance cannot be supported. This will also check the accuracy of the data retrieval system. In the event of a failure, ability to retrieve relevant information is important when traceability, assignment of cause, and identification of similar potential time bombs already in the possession of customers may become vital. The degree to which you check your vendor's records should only be enough to make you feel confident of his recordkeeping.

Let's clarify the foregoing. If you pick a complex assembly, just ask for records of only one leg of the assembly. If, in your opinion, there are too many anomalies, reject the system. If there are no anomalies, accept the system. If you are not convinced one way or another, pick another leg to trace.

Do not try to trace every single step. You are trying to evaluate the working effectiveness of the data keeping system, not the acceptability of a single piece of hardware. To sum up this phase: Choose a significant number of observations so that you may make a judgment as to the acceptability of the vendor's records system. If you need to take too many samples before you can decide, this indicates a weak or indifferent records system.

Avoid the type of surveys in which you, as the potential customer, examine in minute detail all records so as to identify each and every discrepancy that has existed. The supplier may correct everything you identify but assume no responsibility for the correction of defects that may have been missed by your evaluation. Keep in mind that you are trying to identify actual and potential problem areas. It is up to the supplier to correct these and all other areas in which there may be similar conditions. You are after the core of the record system.

Up to this point, we have been philosophizing about the conduct of a survey of a record system. Now, let's consider the specifics of actually looking at the records and how to evaluate the supplier after examination of the records.

Are the records neat? Scribbled records, if legible, are not cause for reflection; illegible records are cause for rejection. Are changes to records made properly? If a single line crosses out original data but does not obliterate it, and the change is initialed by a responsible person, such changes may be acceptable. Other ways suggest sloppy practices and hint of "cooking the books."

Are all blocks filled in on printed forms? Dashes or n/a (not applicable) are acceptable. Ignoring the blanks consistently may indicate failure to comply with requirements. Dashes or n/a suggest that the inspector has considered the requirements and acted accordingly.

Is the retrieval system timely and adequate? Unavailability or lost records may suggest an inadequate system. Speedy retrieval indicates an accurate filing system run by competent personnel.

Are variable data being recorded? Lack of variable data is not in itself cause for rejection unless it is in violation of the specific contractual requirements. However, its presence is usually a sign of a professional quality system, and should be noted favorably by the auditor.

What is the *quality* of these data? If the exact value is being recorded conspicuously often for a given parameter, particularly if it is just within an agreed limit, the data should be questioned. Perhaps it is a case of inspectors "flinching"; perhaps the measuring equipment is calibrated too coarsely. You would normally expect most data to show some kind of unbiased distribution curve. Often, you can picture the distribution mentally as you review these data. Refer back to original data. Reproduced data can hide many sins, such as transposition errors, incorrect formulas, and simple calculation mistakes.

Are the files current? A large backlog of unfiled data may include a lack of personnel, concern, or genuine quality activity. Just collecting data is not quality control.

Most important, are the data used to influence product quality? Most contracts with supplier from primary contractors will not normally call for detailed variables data, quality cost trend analysis, control charts, etc., but much of this will appear in plants that have an underlying commitment to quality. Maintenance of data to verify inspection status is required to protect hardware integrity. The use of data of the foregoing kinds to adjust the quality plan for achieving the most economical cost balance identifies a true professional system. So you should give serious consideration to the effective use of quality data in a supplier's record system.

Closing Conference

The closing conference is your final contact with the supplier's management group before you leave his plant after the survey. Take time to prepare your presentation before the conference. Be specific on discrepancies you found during your survey. Write them down in descending order of importance. Be prepared to explain each one in terms of deficiencies and discrepancies.

In many cases you may need to classify the discrepancies found. Items critical versus your requirements that must be corrected before moving forward in the relationship need to be stated as such. Other major items found or noted during the survey are the next category to be discussed. Unlike critical items, which would place the product at risk, these are unusually major systems faults, which by themselves, do not put product at risk. The final category would be minor errors in system application which would demonstrate inconsistencies in training. These would be noted for the record but no action would be required.

Be quick to point out good points of your potential supplier's quality system so that you keep his confidence. If there is anything particularly laudable, begin your presentation with it. If the supplier cannot understand a discrepancy, be fully prepared to go with him to the area in question to show him. If the supplier fails to understand what is wrong, he may make a futile attempt at correction, perhaps resulting in another discrepancy, which might trigger another survey, perhaps unwarranted.

Do not try to place the blame for discrepancies you find on the supplier group with which you are meeting. It is most probable that the group will have to secure higher management approval to make changes in their quality system.

After discussion, each discrepancy should be noted in writing at the closing conference. Your supplier should give an estimated date for completion of corrective action for each discrepancy. If possible, the discrepancy list should be signed by a representative from the supplier and from the survey group, to indicate that there is a full understanding.

The closing conference can be critical to the health of an ongoing relationship. If the supplier management, the same group you opened with, is assured of your sincerity in building a relationship based on trust and openness, the relationship will grow.

Final Report

The end product of your survey or quality program evaluation should be an understandable final report. A good one effectively communicates the findings, using the original observations to support the conclusions. The report must be an honest, objective summation of your efforts. Even when conveying results that are not always favorable, a professional report, properly written, should be of potential benefit to its recipients. The report should portray the situation dispassionately and give directions for suggested corrective action.

When things are better than you had expected them to be don't forget to give full credit. However, take some care: Unwarranted accolades, as well as improper criticism, destroy the credibility of any report.

An improper report destroys relationships, breeds dissension, and creates mistrust. Such a report may deal with personalities, avoid understanding, and overlook facts. Know your audience. The report must always be in a format and language to suit those for whom it is written. Don't forget that even a formal report can be in narrative style. Unless you are quite sure that most of those who may read your report will understand them, use an absolute minimum of charts, tables, and ratings, and if you do use them, keep them as simple as possible, stressing only the important points. Another way of handling such graphic or tabular material is to refer to them in the body of the report, but transmit them as attachments or appendices to the report itself. Remember the "KISS" principle in report writing: Keep it simple, straightforward.

List all individuals on both teams — don't overlook anyone. Make sure that you get names and positions spelled correctly. A seeming lack of concern here might annoy someone needlessly and make the corrective task much more difficult.

Unlike older, formal style reports, the best modern reports open with a capsule summary of the work carried out and salient recommendations. This lets the busy executive gain an immediate overview of the basic facts. After this, the observations, supporting discussions and, where necessary, detailed recommendations are added. Recommendations should also be given when a specification, procedure, or process is violated. An opinion for a better way to do something may be given as a suggestion or perhaps a comment.

Your report should be sent to the management team with whom you met. Copies should also be sent to the quality control manager and the sales department, if they were not represented. In your own company, copies should be distributed through the QC manager.

The supplier survey will usually indicate an acceptable supplier, a limited supplier, a potentially acceptable supplier, or an unacceptable supplier. Naturally, a report about an acceptable supplier is more pleasant to write than the others. A report about an unacceptable supplier, however, need not be marred by unpleasantness. If the situation with the supplier is such that there was no need or desire to work with them in an improvement process because they were to be dumped, perhaps you should not have even done the survey. Most of the negative surveys will suggest how to rise into at least the potential or limited supplier category. Particularly, in such cases, handling the report with finesse makes all the difference. It can motivate the potential supplier to take suitable corrective action. Grace makes it easier for the limited vendor to accept his limitations, and may even bring the unacceptable supplier to understand his problems and work toward future acceptability.

Don't forget to close your report with expressions of appreciation for the supplier's time, assistance, and cooperation. All suppliers believe that they have rendered you some service.

Follow-Up to Supplier Qualification Surveys

Survey follow-up is carried out to assure satisfactory corrective action has been taken by a supplier who did not qualify at the time of your previous survey visit. You may have to judge if a follow-up visit is warranted, balancing the nature of the findings against the costs of travel and manpower involved. Accompanied by suitable documentation, a report from the supplier of corrective action may be enough.

Keep a genuinely helpful and constructive attitude at all times, and show it by timely support when you deal with all levels of the supplier's personnel. Doing this consistently may be difficult but, as a quality professional, you must do it.

The supplier and your company should have reached agreement during the closing conference on the timetable for corrective action. Documentation of the corrective action schedule should be included in the survey report, and the formal supplier response. You must thoroughly review the survey report and the formal response before a follow-up visit.

Contact the supplier and arrange a mutually agreeable date for the follow-up visit. Schedule a date for the follow-up visit as soon as possible after the execution and reported completion of required corrective action. Make sure that all required corrective action has been completed. If corrective action has not been taken within the required time, your management's policy should provide directions for suitable alternative action.

The audit team cannot assume that the audit is complete until there is objective evidence that the proper corrective action has been completed. This, however, does not absolve the audited organization of its accountability to correct the deficiency.

Show a positive attitude during the follow-up visit. Your supplier has told you he carried out certain corrective actions you agreed on. You are there to verify that the corrective actions have been taken satisfactorily. If all corrective actions are acceptable and no additional problems become known, the supplier should qualify as an *approved supplier*.

If you cannot verify adequate corrective actions, consider the following:

1. If the supplier has made an effort to comply but has not met your requirements, you may have a communication problem. Review the survey report and reported corrective action with the responsible vendor personnel.

2. If requirements have not been satisfactorily fulfilled, the supplier should be advised that he has failed an *approved supplier* status. Mutually agreeable alternatives should be arranged before a visit, and the supplier should be advised accordingly.

You may encounter a situation where the supplier has unique capabilities important to your company, but does not have the resources to invest to provide the quality assurance specified. If possible, the follow-up report should include suggestion(s) for alternative controls, or for direct assistance to the supplier to overcome certain conditions. Competent, understanding assistance in critical situations can be a rewarding investment in securing a satisfactory supplier base.

Post-Survey Team Critique

So you've finished another survey. Congratulations are in order. . .or are they? More than one team, after a survey, has faced that question. How can you answer it? Probably, one of the best ways is to do a team critique.

You carry out a critique to increase the professional competence of the surveyors. It may be tough to face, but the recognition of an individual's or a team's shortcomings is the first necessary step in correcting them. Hopefully, individual or team improvement will be noticed by your management and by the individuals and groups your surveyors contact in your company.

Remind yourself that suppliers about to be surveyed are never happy with what is about to happen. A survey takes time and time means money. A survey improperly handled leaves the supplier open to criticism by the customer. In a supplier plant, each department is expected either to put on a good show or to mislead the evaluators. Such efforts make good surveys difficult. A critique undertaken on the same basis is absolutely worthless.

A proper critique must be realistic. It should consider all the items normally encountered in a supplier or corporate quality survey. The chapter headings of this manual, given below, form an excellent list of subjects to consider in your team critique.

- Goals of a Survey
- Preparation for the Survey
- Team Organization
- Use of Quantification in the Evaluation Format
- Opening Conference
- What to Look for in the Quality Program
- How to Gain the Most from a Plant Tour Including Proprietary Data and Areas
- Evaluation of a Record System
- Closing Conference
- Final Report
- Follow-Up to Supplier Qualification Surveys
- Post-Survey Team Critique
- International
- Supplier Information and Reassurance

A critique by an individual or a team can be a highly emotional activity, so do it in a professional way; reduce emotion and increase effectiveness. Just as in all quality control operations, you must identify nonconformities and weaknesses, rather than blame individuals for weaknesses and inadequacies.

Timing of the critique can help set the proper frame of mind. A critique cannot be effective as a crash program or after some disaster. One good time is shortly after completing a survey when details are still fresh in mind and before the next one is scheduled.

It is probably true there is no perfect product, drawing, or specification. Likewise, there is no perfect survey or supplier, or customer; and there really can be no perfect evaluators. The critique is a search for self-improvement. Individuals or teams who believe they cannot improve their operation are probably poor rather than good.

Therefore, as individuals, we must expect that a critique is going to point out areas for improvement and change. Such is the purpose of a critique. What was good yesterday may not be good enough tomorrow. All surveys look for improvements and ways of making them.

In a critique it is important that unsatisfactory results be identified. It is equally important that areas where improvement can be achieved also be identified. The one often means the other! Identification of areas that can be improved is the purpose of the critique. They are not the causes. It is necessary that the methods for improvement also be identified so that the individuals can improve their performance and increase their efficiency, effectiveness, and the usefulness of the survey.

As an example, the critique may disclose that in a recent survey the reliability tests and results were not properly evaluated. Why did this happen? Were the individuals and perhaps the whole team inattentive? Did they have insufficient training in reliability methods, procedures, and statistics?

Another question might well be: Why were the records not completely and properly evaluated? Were they available to the members of the team or the individual doing the survey — the same people now doing a critique? Was it carelessness, or failure to realize the importance of this area? Was this poor planning?

In conducting a critique it is essential that the problem and not the people be evaluated. This is a self-searching process to find a way to improve the operation.

A critique, to be worthwhile, just like other data analysis situations, requires honesty and integrity. It is not a procedure aimed at finding excuses, but rather at finding areas of the program where major improvements can be effected. This may point to a study course in some particular area. Perhaps just a review with someone at the plant as to what is needed can provide insight that can be developed by home study material. An evaluator cannot be an expert in every field, nor necessarily as expert as someone who is conducting a particular kind of operation. However, the evaluator must have sufficient insight to recognize when things are patently wrong and when things appear to be done properly.

At the end of the critique, a list of areas needing improvement should emerge. Next is deciding how to obtain improvement in each named area. In some areas, provision of training and a program of study, counseling, or management consultation may be indicated. In other instances, it may become obvious that the next survey team should include a specialist when specific specialities are likely to arise or need to be judged in the survey. In any event, plans must be formalized and a commitment made to carry them through and improve the quality of performance of surveys.

As an alternative to the team critique, a peer review similar to that used for design reviews should be considered. In a supplier survey communication is of prime importance. The form of the critique should be a confrontation situation in which the survey team defends its report and survey action to a peer group in its own company. The peer group should be drawn from the purchasing and production staff who would deal with the new supplier. They should have access to the history of the survey and copies of the proposed final report before the meeting.

The survey team must present its report and support its conclusions to this group plus a review chairman supported by two observers. The plant team is then free to question the survey team or each member on specific recommendations or conclusions from the report. The inhouse staff will have to finally accept or reject the report as a useful addition to their working information.

The chairman and observers record significant points presented by both teams and produce an analysis of the proceedings after review. This method of inhouse evaluation and improvement has proved most useful in many design fields, in value engineering, and other situations where communication and action resulting from communication is vital.

The peer group gains from its exposure to the survey team which actually visited and measured the capabilities of the potential supplier. The review makes contact a little easier and the people in the supply source a little more three dimensional.

Finally, the survey team sees the impact of its report on the other half of its own operation. The survey team members have to reason out why things were done and conclusions drawn. It is a satisfactory method of learning provided the chairman and observers ensure that the confrontation is properly conducted and does not degenerate to personalities.

International

Up to this point, discussion has focused on how to deal with the survey of a potential supplier in your own country. When you have to consider suppliers abroad, then you are involved in the international sphere, and you may need a few tips on how to proceed.

Quality assurance has developed rapidly in Europe and Japan, where it is recognized as an important part of export or international sales. When your company has commitments that may involve evaluation of international sources of production, be careful to check what information may be available to you from official or quasi-official bodies.

Most developed countries have state-sponsored organizations responsible for interfacing with foreign business interests, and in this sense you are the foreign interest. These organizations can usually supply product and manufacturing quality references and approvals to expedite sales and maintain their national image.

In Eastern Europe, this organization is sure to be an arm of the state. It may be necessary to obtain the assistance of your government representative in a particular country to make initial contact to get product or manufacturing system verification of quality assurance procedures or practices. The right contact may be a commercial or industrial attaché or representative in the country with which you have to deal.

Where the prospective supplier is located in a NATO or Western-oriented country, contacts should be established with trade ministries, standards institutions, or professional organizations in quality work, to get information on local quality practices, which are sometimes surprisingly good. Most countries have both certification and accreditation procedures which are applied to local quality assurance or testing organizations, usually backed by a national surveillance program to make valid evaluation data available to you. Use such sources whenever possible. In most cases, your professional affiliations will be able to give you information on how to go about contacting indigenous groups in whichever country your company plans to do business at a given time.

Quality assurance is much more formalized outside of continental North America than it is within. Be sure to benefit from any bona fide source of evaluation data available to your organization from such national bodies. Although it may be a costly mistake to assume that some given quality information from abroad is fully equivalent to one you are familiar with, it is by no means rare to discover that, in certain fields of quality accreditation, suppliers abroad may have to regularly meet standards that would strain some of your domestic suppliers to the limit.

Just as with a quality survey of a domestic supplier, treat quality accreditation information abroad with the same open attitude. It may save you from accepting as qualified a supplier who is not, and it may also save you from rejecting a supplier who is more highly qualified than any you might find at home.

The rapid progress being made in most industrialized or newly industrializing countries is astonishing. They are installing all of the sophisticated quality processes which makes international surveys pleasant and easy.

Supplier Information and Reassurance

So you are going to take part in a supplier survey — but it's your plant that is being surveyed. How do you get ready for the survey? First of all, relax and remember that tens of thousands of surveys take place every year. You are not alone.

You may be surveyed by competent quality professionals, perhaps someone who has read this manual. Because you have read it too, you have an idea of what to expect. It would also be useful for you to review *Procurement Quality Control*[3], as well as any specific standards as might apply, such as C1-1985,[1] MIL-Q-9858,[4] ANSI/ASQC Q90-1987,[2] or others. In short, start by arming yourself with knowledge. Know what the surveyor may be seeking.

The next step is to make a realistic appraisal of your plant's quality situation. Do you have a good quality system, or don't you? If the answer is "No," it's almost certainly too late to build one before the survey date. Your best bet is to tell your own management clearly of existing deficiencies. Try to sell management on support of a QC program. Then, when a survey team shows up, learn as much as you can, and take your lumps. Point out that your management has given the support for necessary corrective action. It's foolish to try to hide true facts from a competent evaluator. He'll almost surely find out, and you'll look even worse.

If you have a good system, stand pat. It may not be perfect but nothing ever is. Doubtless the evaluator will find deficiencies somewhere, and you may end up debating necessary corrective action. Don't make the mistake of trying to dress up the operation with a lot of one-time-only spit and polish. Such effort is sure to make your operation look artificial. A competent evaluator knows what a work-a-day facility looks like. He'll rarely be impressed by a "snow job," and may instead become suspicious and wonder what and how much you are trying to cover up.

Make sure that the key people have been thoroughly briefed and their schedules will permit them to be available at the time of the survey for introductions and to answer questions pertaining to their functions. Have an organization chart available. Most QC manuals have charts you can use for models. These charts can be presented to the survey team to inform them who carries out which function in your plant. Also, ensure that documentation that should be available is available.

Recognize that no two systems are alike. Know your own system and how it works. Don't be afraid to defend your system if it really does work. A competent evaluator is interested in new techniques and new ideas. But don't be so defensive that you are unwilling to learn from him if he lets you know of a better idea!

It is not out of place to extend a modest show of professional courtesy to the survey team. He, or they, represents a potential purchaser, which means sales and income for your firm. The survey team will almost surely appreciate the availability of a little office space. Some hospitality, such as a lunch, is not out of line.

References

1. ANSI/ASQC C1-1985. *Specifications of General Requirements for a Quality Program.* Milwaukee: American Society for Quality Control, 1985.

2. ANSI/ASQC Q90-1987 Series. *Quality Management and Quality Assurance Standards.* Milwaukee: American Society for Quality Control, 1987.

3. ASQC Customer-Supplier Technical Committee. *Procurement Quality Control,* 4th ed. James L. Bossert, ed. Milwaukee: ASQC Quality Press, 1988.

4. Department of Defense MIL-Q-9858A. Washington: Government Printing Office, 1965.

Certification Presentation Agenda

The following agenda is a guide for presentations of the certified supplier plaque at the supplier's plant.

A. Meet in a room to get acquainted.

B. Supplier introduces all principals, presenters from both the customer and the supplier.

C. Corporate quality states the highlights of the quality improvement process, where certification fits in, requirements for certification, and what certification means to customer plants.

D. Purchasing manager comments on relationship, length of time, etc.;

restates the importance of certified suppliers for cost, quality, delivery goal achievement, etc.; and comments on supplier's achievements.

E. *Lead plant* SQA engineer comments on the quality relationship with the supplier, pertinent historical notes, supplier's performance in the field of quality, etc.

F. VP of purchasing comments on the importance of a quality improvement program to customer and suppliers and challenges the supplier to continuous improvement beyond certification to impact on cost, quality, and delivery. Presents plaque.

G. Supplier response to certification award and challenge for continuous improvement.

Index

The late **Richard "Rick" A. Maass** was manager of Supplier Quality Assurance for the Pharmaceutical Products Division of Abbott Laboratories in North Chicago, Illinois. A past chairman of the ASQC Customer-Supplier Technical Committee, Rick authored two books published by Quality Press about customer/supplier human relations, *For Goodness' Sake, Help!* and *World Class Quality — An Innovative Prescription for Survival.*

John O. Brown is currently manager of worldwide quality assurance/supplier development for the Cummins Engine Company. He managed a multi-national, multi-plant supplier quality function, including program design, training, and coordination among 17 manufacturing and assembly locations. John has an MBA degree and is a member of the Customer-Supplier Division of ASQC.

A quality consultant with Eastman Kodak Company, **James L. Bossert's** current responsibilities involve the implementation of the "soft" quality technologies, including QFD, benchmarking, and quality planning. The editor of *Procurement Quality Control,* Jim is the author of *QFD: A Practitioner's Approach,* soon to be published by Quality Press. He is a member of the Customer-Supplier Division of ASQC.